The Art of Rug I

Learning How to N

Dueep Jyot Singh

Learning Series

Mendon Cottage Books

JD-Biz Publishing

Download Free Books!

http://MendonCottageBooks.com

Our books are available at

1. Amazon.com
2. Barnes and Noble
3. Itunes
4. Kobo
5. Smashwords
6. Google Play Books

Download Free Books!

http://MendonCottageBooks.com

Table of Contents

Introduction

I was just browsing through my own personal library, looking at all the vintage craft books, but I did not find a book with instructions on how to make rugs. I could make Victorian crochet doilies, knitted mittens, scarfs, some articles of clothing called fascinators, and even socks and knickerbockers, but what about rugs?

It is only later that I found out that according to the Victorians rug making was not considered to be a genteel occupation, which could be indulged in by the daughters and wives of gentlemen. These languishing ladies would sit in front of the embroidery frame, plying a needle, while dining of strawberries and cream, no doubt, while rug making was done by people of lower social strata.

Nevertheless, we are fortunate that we have stopped thinking of such idiotic considerations in order to make rugs. So this book is going to tell you all about the art of rug making, and you are going to let your creativity loose in making these amazingly beautiful items for your home.

Tools Required

Many of these tools can be found in rummaging through your old cupboards, if your grandmothers/mothers were into these crafts. Incidentally, during the Great Depression, and in the 30s and 40s, everybody was in rug making of some sort or the other, and so you may find some of them very easily, others can be found in auction lots on eBay. Look for lots, so that you can get lots of items at one time, like I did as far as my collection of rug hooks, latch hooks, Brown's patented shaggy rag tools, bodgers, proddies/proggies, punch needles, and rug guns went.

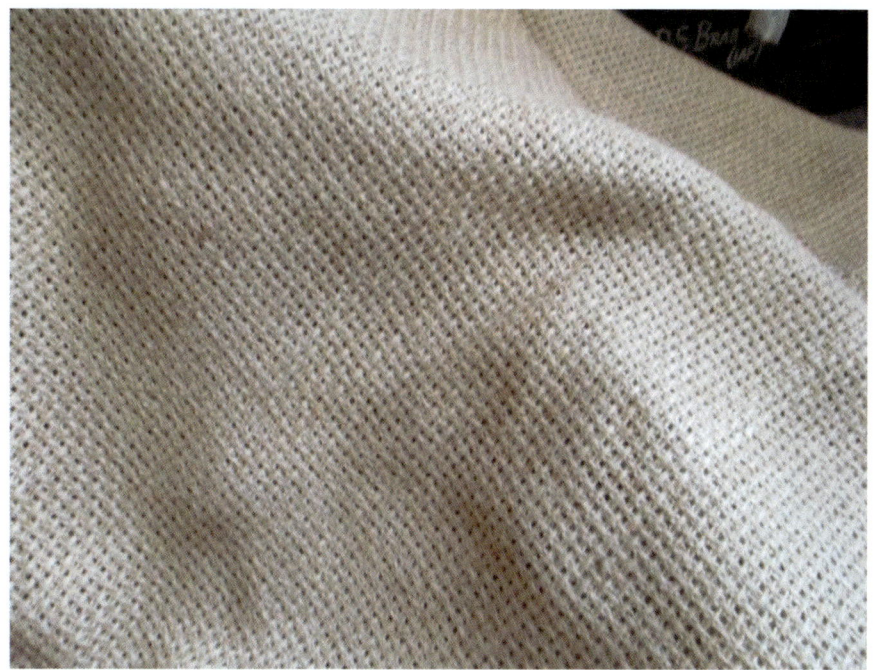

Jute sacking, for the backing of the rug

Remember that originally rugs were made by people who did not have lots of money to spend on supplies. That is why they use their own ingenuity to make their rugs. So I am going to do the same thing, and even though I have some original ancient vintage rug making tools, I am going to teach you how to make your own rug making tools, as far as possible.

A handmade rug is going to be a thing of beauty and a joy forever. Down the ages, rugs have been made different ways, by using latch hooks, bodgers, crochet knooking needles, and patented rug making tools.

Along with that, you are going to need a stiff material as a background on which you are going to do the rug hooking. This can either be canvas or if you want, you can use jute sacking, like I do. After all this sacking has been used through the ages, by people all over the world to make these rugs.

Knooking Needles

Along with that, if you want to make your own knooking needles and crochet needles, you can always invest in a woodcarving set of 12 pieces. As far as I believe, it is a once-in-a-lifetime buy, and it is going to serve you well, throughout your life, especially when you want to do a little bit of creative activity on wood yourself.

I got it on eBay on a buy it now offer of $3.56 HERE
http://tinyurl.com/qzyzv7w

Incidentally, when you get these tools, they are not going to be in sharpened condition. You will have to do the sharpening, because for shipping reasons, they are left unsharpened. I was rather annoyed when I got this set, because hey, why were they not sharpened? And then logic struck especially for safety purposes and you can see the blade side, which needs to be sharpened. According to the requirement of your tool, you can do the grinding and sharpening.

You can watch a video HERE **http://tinyurl.com/zmr242q** explaining how to do this.

This is how you sharpen the tools, even though I have not managed to find a really good diamond stone yet. I sharpened these tools on an ancient whetstone and it served the purpose.

I am carving a crochet needle with one of the chisels. This needs to be done very carefully, especially when you are doing it for the first time, so that you do not have any nicks and cuts when the chisels slips. This is how you do it, watch HERE **http://tinyurl.com/npuewbu**

After you have carved a crochet needle to your satisfaction, use a drill to make a small eyehole on the other part of the handle. There you are, you have a Knooking needle now Knit+ Hook- Knook) . It should have been crochet plus hook, but the word "Crook" has been already gone into popular vocabulary. You can also make this Knooking needle's eyelet by using a sharp knife, as long as you are careful.

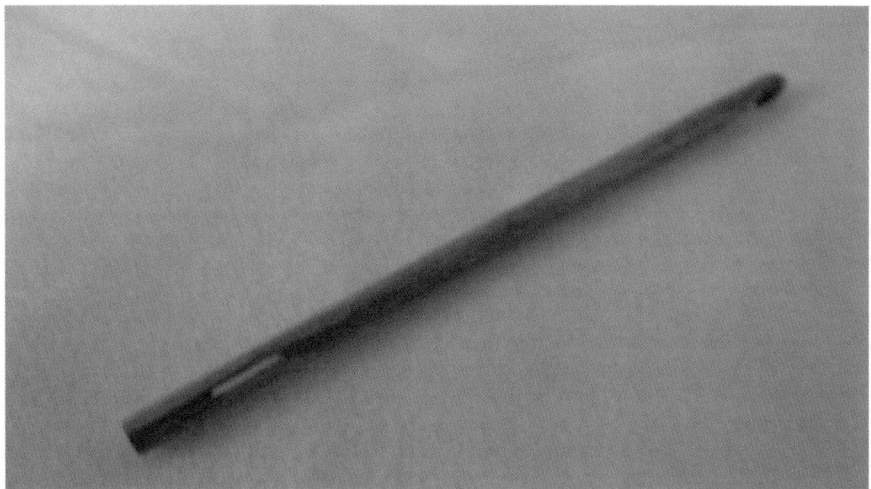

This needle is used for locker needle hooking, which we are going to learn later on.

Latch Rug Hooking

This is how a latch rug hook looks close up.

This is made up of a wooden handle, with a bent hook, and a latch, in which you are going to insert the piece of cut wool. If you look at vintage rug making kits, you are going to find that they are going to come with wool already cut.

That means all you need to do is get your frame ready, fasten your piece of base material – either canvas or jute – to the frame and there you are, you are ready for rug making.

A collection of vintage latch rug hooks

Frames

Firstly, you should make sure that the frames are steady and sturdy, and are capable of holding your canvas firmly. These frames can be as large or as small as you wish.

Here are 2 frames standing on a piece of jute sacking, which I asked of a shopkeeper. In many parts of the world, jute is still used very commonly for storage purposes and it is the best natural fiber on which to make your rug.

So how did I get the frames? I just bought small tables, large enough, which could cover my lap if I sat cross legged upon the floor, plying my hook from underneath.

Remember that it should be small enough for your hands to move under comfortably. Large rug frames are unwieldy, – I have one which is 3.5' x 6' and I use it for weaving carpets. But that is when I am in the mood to do so! It is too much of an effort especially when I do not intend marketing or selling them.

The good thing about this small table is when I turn it upside down, and knock out all the nails holding the flat surface to the wooden frame, I am going to have a really good piece of wood, which I am going to make into a weaving loom further on in this book. You can weave carpets, rugs, and whatever you want, on weaving looms.

So now you that you have got your frames settled, you just take the canvas, stretch it tightly over the frame, and pin it into the wood of the frame with ordinary drawing pins, – you may need to put in a little bit of effort here, and a hammer comes in handy.

Remember that the pinning is going to be done in the area of the canvas, which is not a part of your design. That pinned area is going to be made up in the end with a little bit of hemming, to tuck in the loose edges and give your rug a professional look.

There are normally 3 steps when you do the latching. Latching is done with pieces of precut wool – this process is going to be shown further on – and the demonstration is being shown on a large piece of canvas, so that it can be seen clearly.

Firstly, you are going to find a weft thread. It moves from selvedge to selvedge. Selvedge is the edge of the canvas, where all the threads are gathered up. In the picture down below, you can see the selvedge right on top of the picture, but as it is all around my particular piece of canvas, I am doing the latching through a weft thread.

Push your latch hook from above, under the canvas by pushing the hook underneath it.

Now you are going to keep the ends level. Fold a wool length in half over the hook and pull it towards you. You are now drawing the wool loop under the weft thread.

Push the hook forward again so that the latch falls open. Turn the hook slightly to the right placing the cut ends of the wool over the hook. You can see how you are going to do it in the diagram picture on the extreme right. The latch hook is open and the wool is being placed/pulled through the hook.

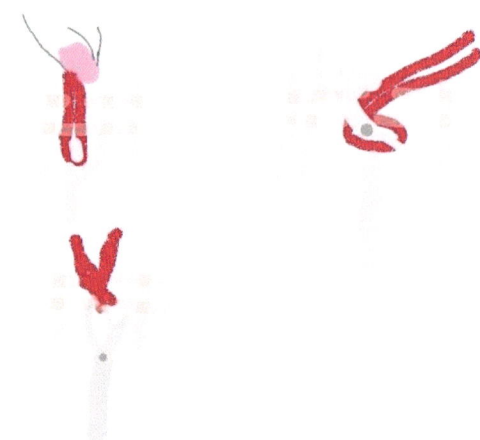

Now fully hook towards you, letting the latch close automatically as it comes through the loop. Pull the ends of the wool firmly so that the knot is formed and firm.

You can see that this look is the shaggy look, especially when you are making a rug with a deep "pile". This is normally made with lots of pieces of precut wool, and it is also made up of little pieces of cloth snipped into pieces.

Precut wool

There are many ways in which you can cut the wool in equal lengths, and here are some really interesting vintage useful tools, which have been used down the ages for cutting this wool.

The Patwin wool cutting vintage machine has been around for more than 80 years. I found this collection by rummaging through online sales for the best bids I could find. Three I got from Australia and one I got from the UK. That is because I think this is the UK-based company started by Paton and Baldwin.

The instructions for using this tool are very easy. Turn it upside down, and it is going to tell you where to insert the piece of wool so that you can pull it from above. After that, you are going to wind the wool through the other hole and thread it through the eyelet on top of the winding handle.

It instructs you how to turn the winding handle so start cranking in a clockwise direction.

And there you are, with wool of the same size is cut immediately. The wool is not going to come out from any easily available hole. You just have to pull it away from the area around which you have wound your yarn. After doing the cranking 20 or more times, I got a bit het up, the first time I used it because I imagined the wool dropping away automatically as it was being cut. It does not. Collect the wool, and put it in different packets, ready for use, for when you begin your project.

Apart from these classic wool cutters Paton had their own wool cutters made out of wood in which there was a deep groove. You would slip your scissors inside the groove, and cut the wool which had been wound around the wood.

In the same manner, here is another vintage wool winder which works really well.

You do the winding of the wool in a clockwise direction, after knotting the corner of the yarn around the wood.

You can make as many of the woolen rounds as you wish, depending on the amount of wool you need.

The cutting of the wool is just going to be by inserting a pair of scissors through the groove on top, and scissoring through.

Now that we know how to cut wool easily, let us start on another project in the making up of rugs, where we are going to use uncut wool. This is called locker needle hooking.

Locker Needle Hooking

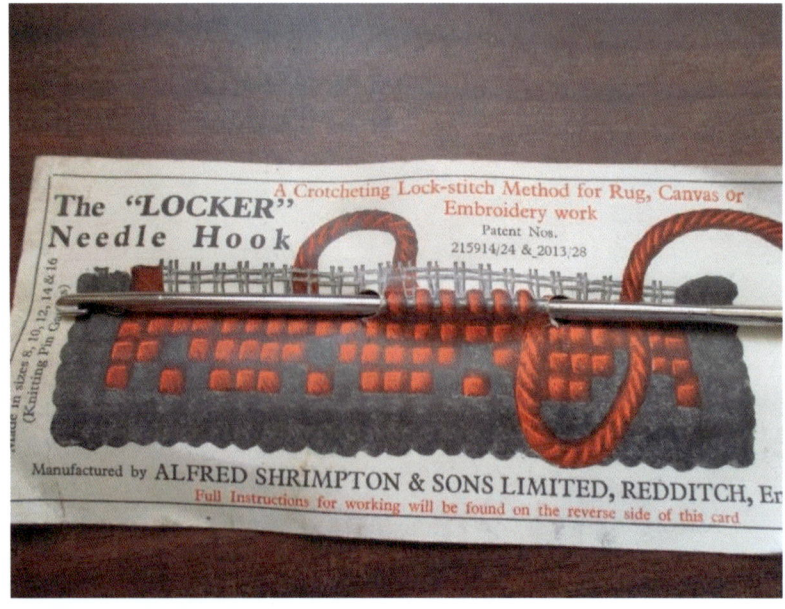

This is also a very interesting way in which you can do the hooking of the rugs, especially when you are using a special rug needle which has a hook on one end and a needle eyelet on the other.

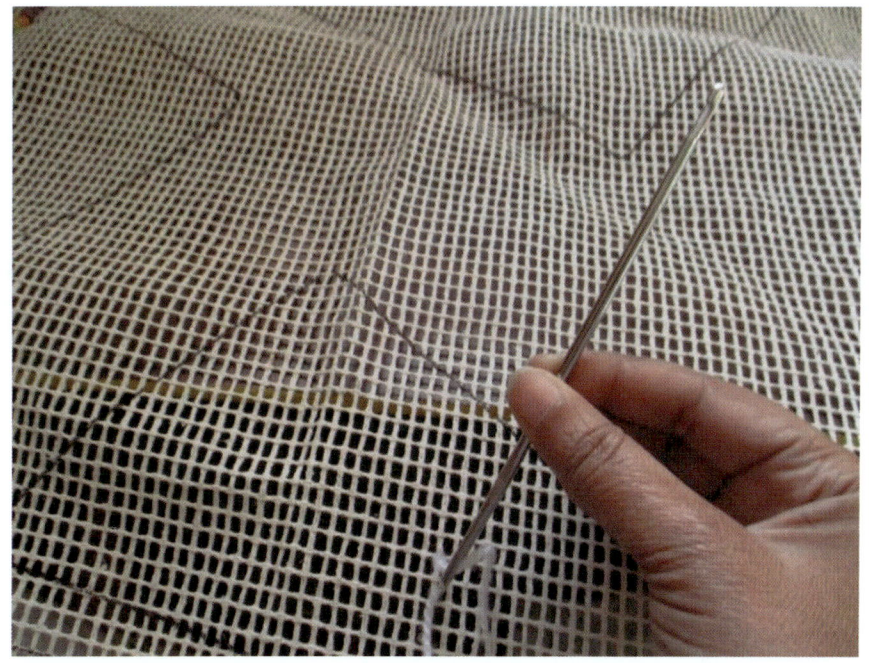

I have just made a crazy design on a piece of canvas, for tutorial purposes, with a fabric pen, and now I am holding up this locking needle with about a yard or so of wool threaded through it. The wood has been knotted at one end, which is going to be holding the thread on the underside of the canvas steadily when I begin the rug knotting process on the top of the canvas.

My fingers can be seen under the canvas with wool which is in a ball. I am going to be using that ball of wool for making my rug.

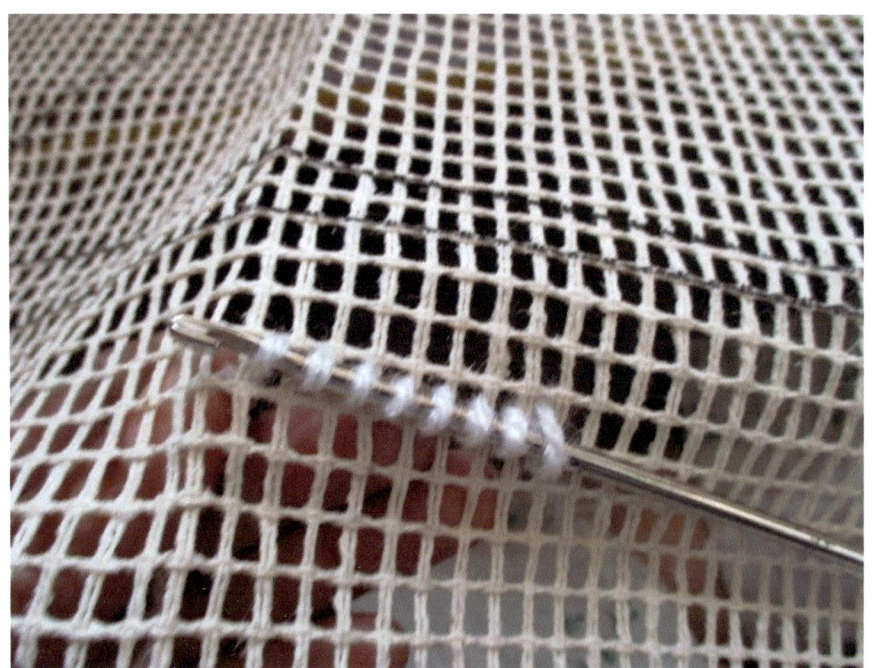

You slip the needle from above, into the hole, wind the yarn over the hook, and draw the loop up above remembering to hold it on your needle. If you know Tunisian crochet, this is very easy to do. We also have a Tunisian Crochet book HERE **http://tinyurl.com/qjgp564** if you want it too.

Once you have a number of loops on your hook, you are going to fix them on the surface of the rug by pulling the needle with its accompanying yarn through the loops.

Remember to fasten this fastening yarn on the underside of the canvas with the help of a knot. Just imagine that you are using a needle and a thread. This is exactly what you are doing, fastening the loops to the cloth with the help of a needle and thread in just one go.

After you have slipped off all the loops of your hook and onto the canvas and fastened it, this is what you are going to get.

I have purposely used a large mesh canvas so that you can see the effect of different plies of wool on different sized canvases. This wool is a wishy-washy 2 ply wool. Below, you can see the results of 6 ply wool on a large meshed canvas.

This wool has been knotted into place. You can see the knotting/holding thread going through the loops vertically on the bottom picture. You can also see the thread below in the picture on the bottom, which is going to be used with the hook to continue the project. This thread is attached to a ball of wool. Continue this until all the wool on your needle has finished. After that, thread another couple of yards of wool on your needle, attach it to any loop on the under portion of the canvas, near the end of the last loop on which you worked and continue.

Apart from this method of making woolen rugs, there is another way of making shabby pile rugs. Here we are not going to be using pieces of precut wool, but we are going to be looping loops with uncut wool.

Pile Rug

You need a little bit of care, when you are doing this project, because there is no way in which you can hold the thread into place. We are just lifting the thread by inserting the needle from above, looping the yarn under the canvas and then pulling the loop up. This loop is not placed on the hook but left as it is on the canvas.

People normally finish a project with this particular method, and then attach a stiff backing on the back of the rug in order to keep the stitches in place.

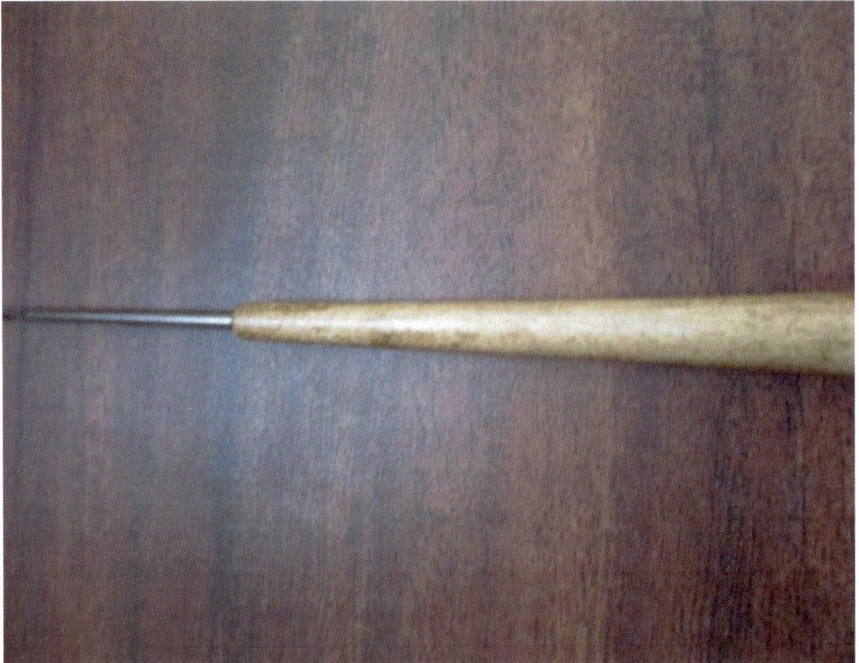

This is the hooking needle which is used in such a project. It is like a long crochet hook, inserted in a wooden handle.

Making Rugs with Rug Guns

Rug guns have been all the rage since the late 19th century, in order to make rugs on a really small meshed background like jute.

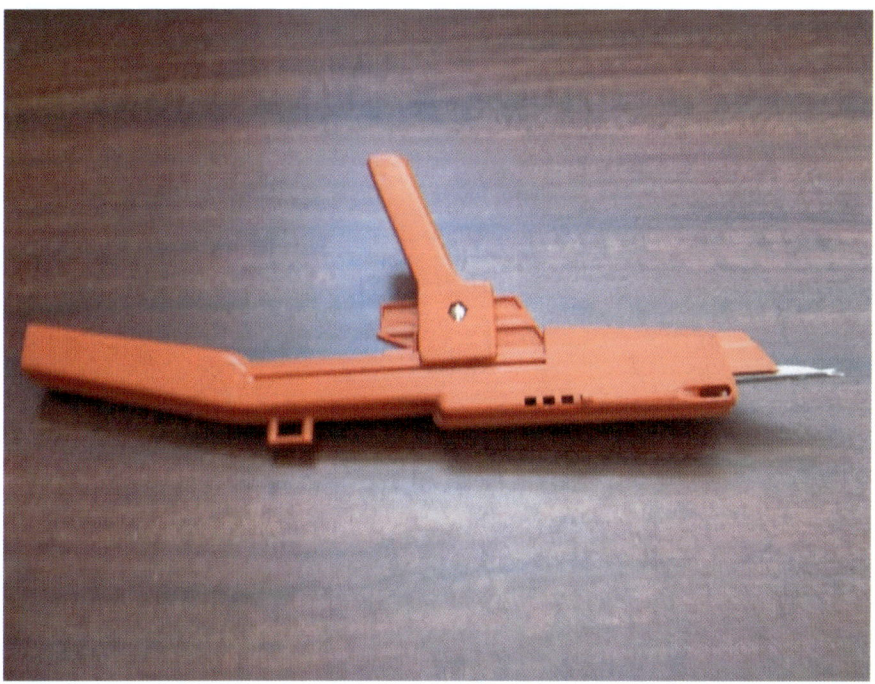

This is a Ronco rug gun which was very popular in the 60s and 70s. Looks a bit like a machine gun. You are going to thread the thread through the eyelet in the needle after pulling it through that square loop. This loop is for keeping the thread taut.

A Ronco kit has its own plastic frame on which you are going to attach the fabric, which has been printed with the design before hand. My kit had a flowers design, but I was more interested in this rug gun and the frame! This procedure is also known as tufting.

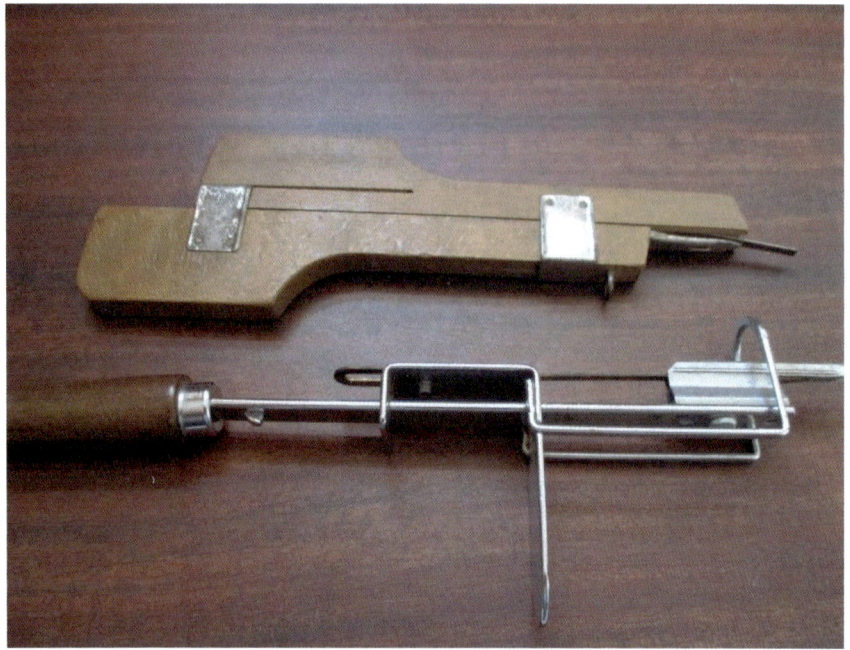

Along with this, here are another 2 vintage rug tufting shuttles going back to the early 1900s to the 1940s. This was when women began to understand that rug making was not a lowly occupation and after the 2nd World War, and during the Great Depression, this was a good way in which warm rugs could be made with the help of leftover wool.

Watch how to do the tufting method HERE
http://tinyurl.com/pavcqp4

Believe it or not, I have tried it out, yes, once you get the hang of tufting, you will be able to go as fast as the video shows. In fact, these experienced workers do about one square foot or more in about an hour's time.

But you have to be certain that the fabric is stretched taut against the frame so that there is no give in the fabric when you are inserting the tufting tool through the jute. Incidentally, it is going to work on its own, you do not have to pull the needle out. It moves to the next mesh automatically. All you have to do is ply the machine-gun lever as fast as you can while moving your hand a little bit over the design in the direction you want the thread to go.

I found this blog **http://tinyurl.com/z3s98w3** really interesting because you can see how the different tools are being used here.

Punching needles and other tools

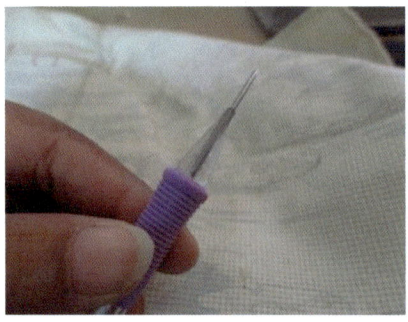

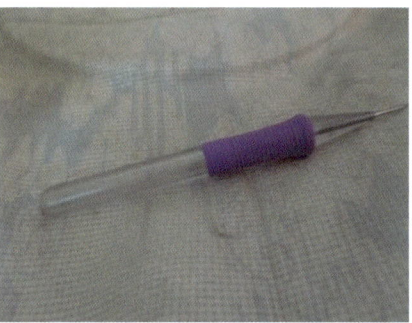

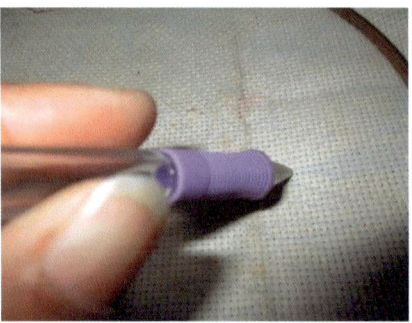

As time went by, people began to look at other easily pliable tools with which the punching could be done. Here, I have a tool called a pictograph punch needle, and I am working on a really old piece of canvas, taken from my grandmother's work box.

These were used when you did not want to use a needle for cross stitching.

A punch needle has a hollow holder in which a needle is fit. Thread the needle through the back of the holder, it normally comes with a needle threader, thread the needle through the eyelet from back to front.

Then start punching your design.

There are other designs in punching needles, and I got this one from Hong Kong, free international shipping, from the seller HERE.

http://tinyurl.com/z48whk2

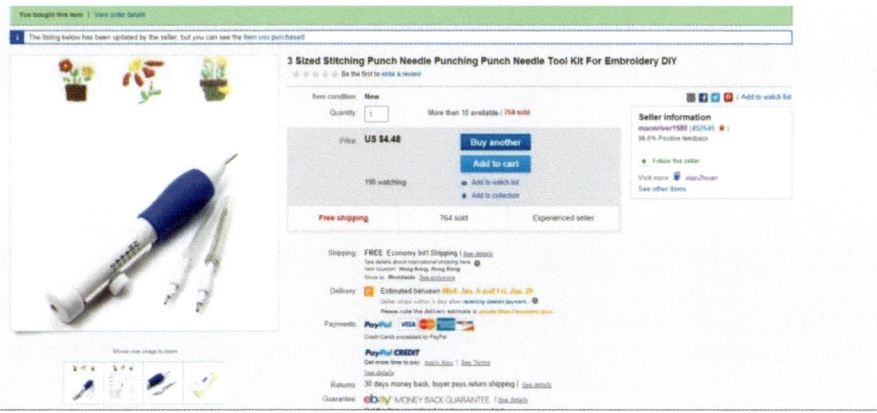

It is possible that you can get a cheaper bargain on eBay, but as the seller has already been confirmed as a person whose items reach their destinations, go right ahead!

HERE **http://tinyurl.com/q49p87m** is an excellent URL for beginners.

Remember that it is very easy to pull out the thread, once the needle has been inserted through the canvas, and pulled out again to make the next loop/stitch. So I found a good way of preserving my work. I just put a thin layer of gum over the stitches at the back of the canvas, and when it was dry and the stitches had stuck fast to the cloth, I covered it with a stiff cloth covering – buckram.

Move the needle away from you and do not pull it out very high above the cloth when you are dipping it in for the next stitch. Also remember that the needle has to go completely through the cloth up to the handle, when you are making the stitches.

Make your own design on your cloth with a piece of tracing paper with carbon under it.

This vintage punch needle is going to work on canvas and help bring up the wool in loops, like the hook did in the pile rugs. It has 2 holes, which means you can have either a small loop or a larger loop.

You can either pull the loop up on the surface of the design or allow the thread to be punched in completely with the help of the punch.

In both the cases, the back portion of the rug is going to look like this. If you want, you can use this side as your shaggy rug surface. I am using a 6 ply wool for this particular project on a large canvas.

Rug Weaving

Now we come to that really amazing and fulfilling skill of rug weaving and carpet weaving which has been around for centuries. A weaver is going to have a professional room, and as I really do not have the space, and money to get a huge loom made for carpets – I have one about 60 years old, which was used by my grandmother to weave carpets – but I really do not have the patience to work on it.

So we are starting on a web weaving frame which we are going to make ourselves.

Do you remember the top of the table, which I had knocked off, when I was showing you the frames for the canvases? This tabletop is going to be used, to make an easily manageable loom.

For this, I just need some nails depending on how large I want my woven fabric to be, and 2 pieces of thick wooden blocks which I am going to nail to that wooden table top.

You can see the nail peeping out on the left top of the picture. It was large enough to go through the wooden block and hold it fast to the tabletop.

Then I used my drill to drill some holes. This makes it easier for me to hammer the nails into the block of wood. These nails are going to hold the thread, which are the warp and the weft.

Some of the sturdy threads are going to be horizontal. This is the warp. The threads that we are going to weave in and out of the warp threads are going to be the weft threads.

I did the marking at an interval of half inch with a wooden marker so that I knew exactly where to drill. Use your smallest drill bit. After all, you do not want the hole to be so large that your nail does not fit in it properly and firmly. Nails moving about all over the place are a bore.

I used 2 pieces of plywood blocks which were left over after another DIY session, so instead of throwing it away, it is being used, to make this web loom.

One plywood block is going to be nailed to the top of your loom, and one to the bottom. Make sure the nails correspond, when you are nailing them on both the blocks because you do not want a lopsided warp, do you?

Getting ready for weaving is done by winding the thread around the nails so that you have one top and one bottom thread around each nail. That means you are going to find 2 threads around each nail. This is helpful, because then you can see which thread is at the top and which thread is at the bottom. This comes in useful when you are winding the shuttle above and under the threads. You can also use a long needle, in which you have threaded the wool. This makes it easier to ply the needle in and out of the warp.

Here is an easy instructive URL, which helps you to start weaving HERE
http://tinyurl.com/j3r9xet

Incidentally, I did not cut the thread into equal sized pieces, because that is a really boring process. Just start at one end, take the thread to the corresponding nail on the other side of the board, bring it back again, thread around the 2nd nail head on the top of the loom, go back to the 2nd nail head at the bottom of the loom and then bring the thread back again to the 3rd nail head on the top of the loom, and so on. Make sure that the thread is tight.

In fact this can be done by hammering nails projecting outwards on the side of the plywood block. After you have come to let us say the first nail top with 2 threads and are ready to loop the 2nd nail, make a loop around the nail extending outside instead. This is going to go over the side of your plywood, down to a nail extending facing you. After that, lift the thread, loop it over the 2nd nail head, go back down to the bottom corresponding 2nd nail head, loop it over the nail extending away from you at the bottom, thus holding the thread fast. You are going to have a starburst of threads at the end of the weaving session. These are going to help make your selvedge.

A little bit of weaving done with some wool with the help of shuttles.

Now let us come to the shuttles. If we do not have long enough needles, shuttles come in useful.

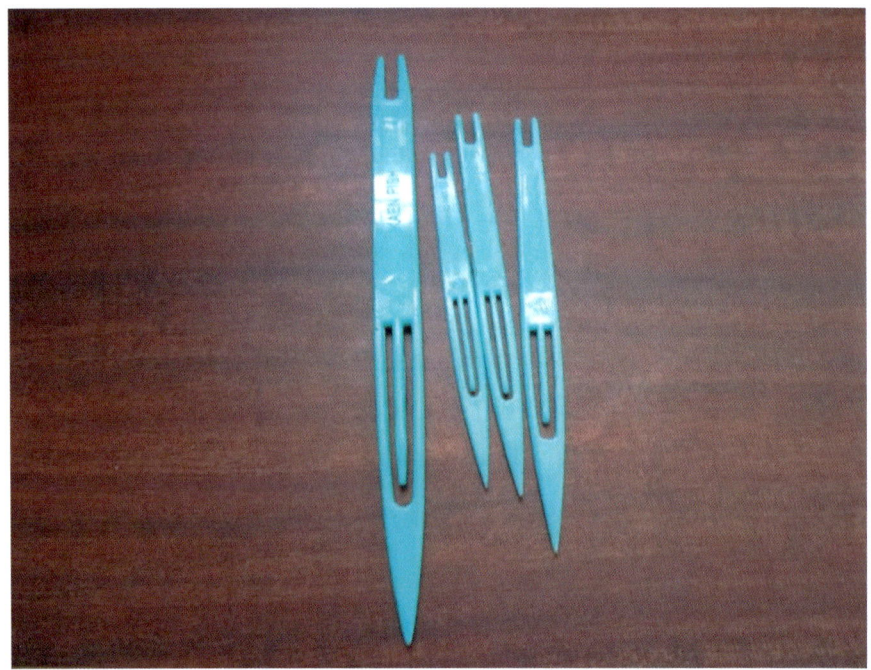

These shuttles came in a group of 5, which I found HERE.

http://tinyurl.com/jblgdf6 The 5th shuttle is attached to the project, I am making in the pictures shown below.

You can get them cheaper from Hong Kong or anywhere else with a little bit of research.

I am threading the shuttle with wool. You are going to hold it firmly in your left hand, after tying a knot to the shuttle center. After that, you are going to pull the wool across the inner portion, wind it anticlockwise, bring the thread down and then loop it through the U-shaped loop. Then pull the thread up again and repeat the procedure. You will soon have a shuttle with lots of old, depending on how much wool you need for your project.

Now we begin weaving the thread in and out of the warp. Thanks to the sharp nose of the shuttle, it is easy for me to thread the wool around the top threads. Have you noticed that I have started the new shuttle line by threading a thread over and under the last thread? That is because this last thread is the one extra thread which I am going to make sure is present when I am making a warp.

For example, if your design says make a warp of 18 threads; you are going to make a warp of 18+1 = 19 threads. The last thread is the thread on which I am going to attach the wool of my shuttle with a sturdy knot, you can see it right there top right, before I started weaving the shuttle over and under.

When you reach the end of your line, you use a ruler or even the shuttle to push the thread closer to its fellow woven threads. You can see that I am doing the pushing and the weaving in and out at the same time.

On the 19th thread, you are going to turn, take your shuttle from above the thread and then below it hold fast and then continue weaving through the rest of the top threads until you have completed another line.

There are plenty of websites, out there which give you free patterns like this very useful one HERE **http://tinyurl.com/ppt4nk7**

It seems it also has some free books with rug making designs in them. So if you do not think this to be a very ambitious project, you can try anything out there on those books.

Use your own ingenuity to make these rugs.

Rag Rugs with Recycled Scraps

Long time ago, when people were more conservative about the materials they own, every scrap of clothing was utilized, even when it was ragged and could not be mended and re-patched and worn, yet once again.

So if you have plenty of clothes, which you want to turn into a rag rug, start right now. Here are some of the tools which you will need in order to cut the rag rug materials from old cloth.

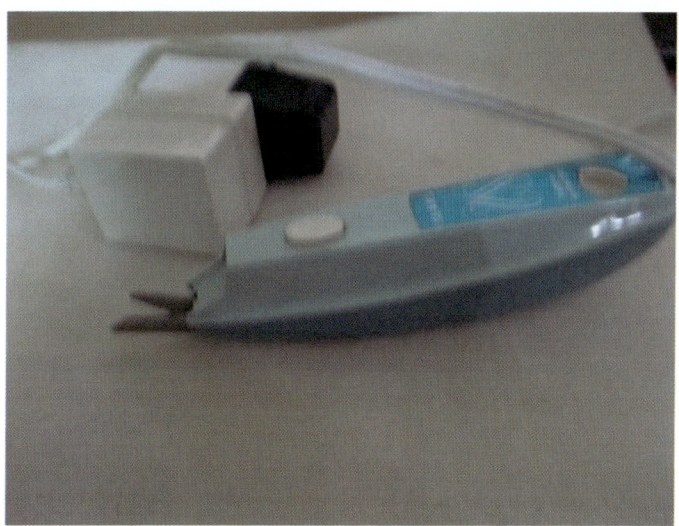

Battery operated scissors, rollerblade cutter and Sears electric 3 speed scissors. The battery operated scissors and the Sears's scissors are vintage, though the rollerblade cutter is available at any craft store.

Use them to cut strips of cloth, if you are crocheting a rag rug, or just small pieces of cloth.

Apart from this, we have these different vintage tools which help you push or prod in the small piece of rag.

 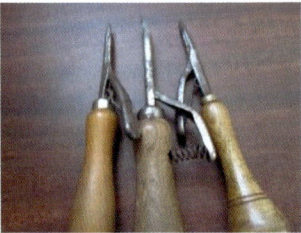 

Heavy iron hook, Brown's patented rag rug tools, and proddy hook

Apart from prodding the piece of rag into the canvas, this proddy hook can also be used to make pile shaggy rugs by hooking the thread from underneath and bringing the thread up in a loop on the top of your canvas.

HERE **http://tinyurl.com/hay89h7** is an interesting URL which you can enjoy. You can use any sharp and pointy instrument to prod the piece of rag into a fabric hole, even though I am using proddies. Use whatever comes to hand.

Here is a pile of cloth, which I have cut into long strips as well as small scraps.

The long strips are going to be crocheted into long braids, which can then be sewn together into crocheted rugs. As long as you have plenty of clothes available, which can be cut into strips, you can never have a dearth of this particular fabric material.

A little bit of effort and you can get a Technicolored rug made up of different fabrics.

HERE **http://tinyurl.com/hay89h7** is an ingenious URL, where you can get the full tutorial on how you can make your own rag rug. You can make it as large and as small as you want. People normally crochet lots of long ropes of fabric, and then use a round needle to stitch them together in rounds.

My way is – You can try experimenting by making a ring of 6 chain, and making it into a circle by slip stitching the first and the 6th chain together. After that you are going to slip stitch into each chain to finish the first round. The next round is going to be made with 2 chains as the initial beginning stitch, and one double crochet into each slip stitch of the 2nd round. This is the 3rd round. For the 4th round, you are going to begin the round with 2 chains – whenever you intend to use double crochet in the row/round, the first stitches of the new row are always going to be 2 chains.

The 4th round is going to have 2 double crochets in each double crochet of the previous round. That means you have 12 double crochets.

Make another round with one double crochet in these 12 double crochets. The 6th round is going to be made up of one double crochet in these 12 double crochets which makes 24 double crochets.

This shows you that every even round is an increasing round. You can do the increasing as you like, by doing one repeated double crochet to every 2 previous double crochets –*one dc, 2 dc*repeated in previous row instead of 2 dc, 2 dc , and so on.

Using a Shaggy Rug Tool

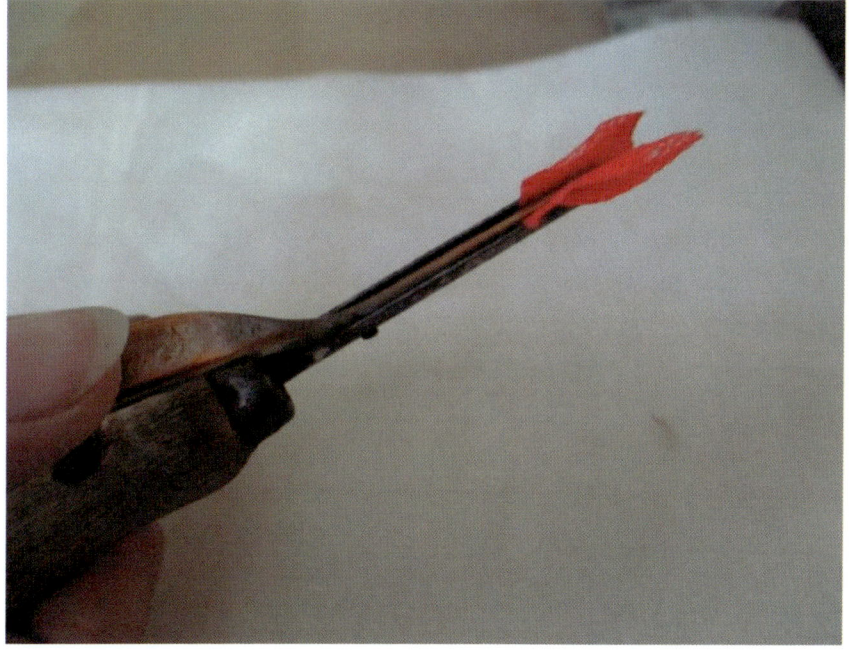

This is another vintage tool, which is used extensively to make shaggy rugs. This URL **http://tinyurl.com/h3ofdq3** is going to give you easy information on how you can do the lag rug making after you have cut pieces of clothes/cloth into manageable pieces. I would suggest the dimensions be of about 2 inches in length, and one and a half inches in width, depending on how thick you want the pile to be. If you want a really thick pile, the width can be 2 ½ or 3 inches in width.

Conclusion

I do hope you have got a lot of tips on how you can begin on rag rug making. After reading the book, you are going to say, what is the matter, you have given me all this information, but you have not given me any project to do. Where are all the projects I can make, through instructions given on a design which I can pick up in this book itself, instead of going online and searching for a design of your own.

Well, my friend, the answer is that I do not know what you would like to do. Would you want to go in for something really challenging at the first instance or would you like a simple project in the initial stages?

You may want to do the crocheted rug in shell stitch. You can find instructions HERE **http://tinyurl.com/z6k5mwu**

Also, this particular page HERE **http://tinyurl.com/y42yhr** is really enjoyable and interesting, especially when you want to look at all the stitches you want to do, in order to create something for the first time. All you need is the time, the energy and the inclination.

And HERE **http://tinyurl.com/p6g7xey** is how you learn how to crochet any pattern you choose.

So when you are making your rag rug with your crocheting needle, you can use any of these video instructions in order to learn the basics, and traditional crochet designs! So take some time out and learn a new skill!

Live Long and Prosper!

Author Bio

Dueep Jyot Singh is a Management and IT Professional who managed to gather Postgraduate qualifications in Management and English and Degrees in Science, French and Education while pursuing different enjoyable career options like being an hospital administrator, IT,SEO and HRD Database Manager/ trainer, movie , radio and TV scriptwriter, theatre artiste and public speaker, lecturer in French, Marketing and Advertising, ex-Editor of Hearts On Fire (now known as Solstice) Books Missouri USA, advice columnist and cartoonist, publisher and Aviation School trainer, ex-moderator on Medico.in, banker, student councilor ,travelogue writer … among other things!

One fine morning, she decided that she had enough of killing herself by Degrees and went back to her first love -- writing. It's more enjoyable! She already has 48 published academic and 14 fiction- in- different- genre books under her belt.

When she is not designing websites or making Graphic design illustrations for clients , she is browsing through old bookshops hunting for treasures, of which she has an enviable collection – including R.L. Stevenson, O.Henry, Dornford Yates, Maurice Walsh, De Maupassant, Victor Hugo, Sapper, C.N. Williamson, "Bartimeus" and the crown of her collection- Dickens "The Old Curiosity Shop," and "Martin Chuzzlewit" and so on… Just call her "Renaissance Woman" - collecting herbal remedies, acting like Universal Helping Hand/Agony Aunt, or escaping to her dear mountains for a bit of exploring, collecting herbs and plants, and trekking.

Check out some of the other JD-Biz Publishing books

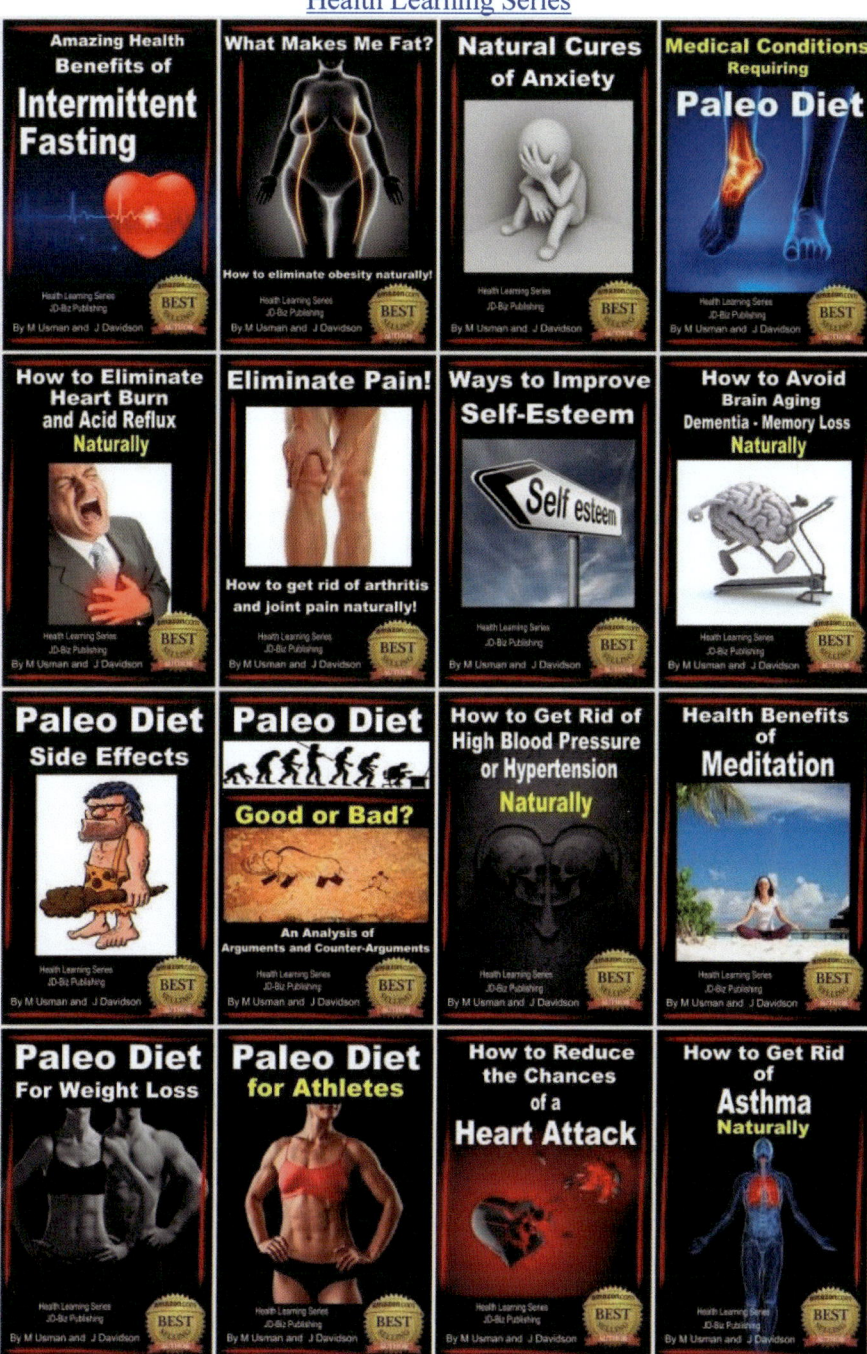

Amazing Animal Book Series

Learn To Draw Series

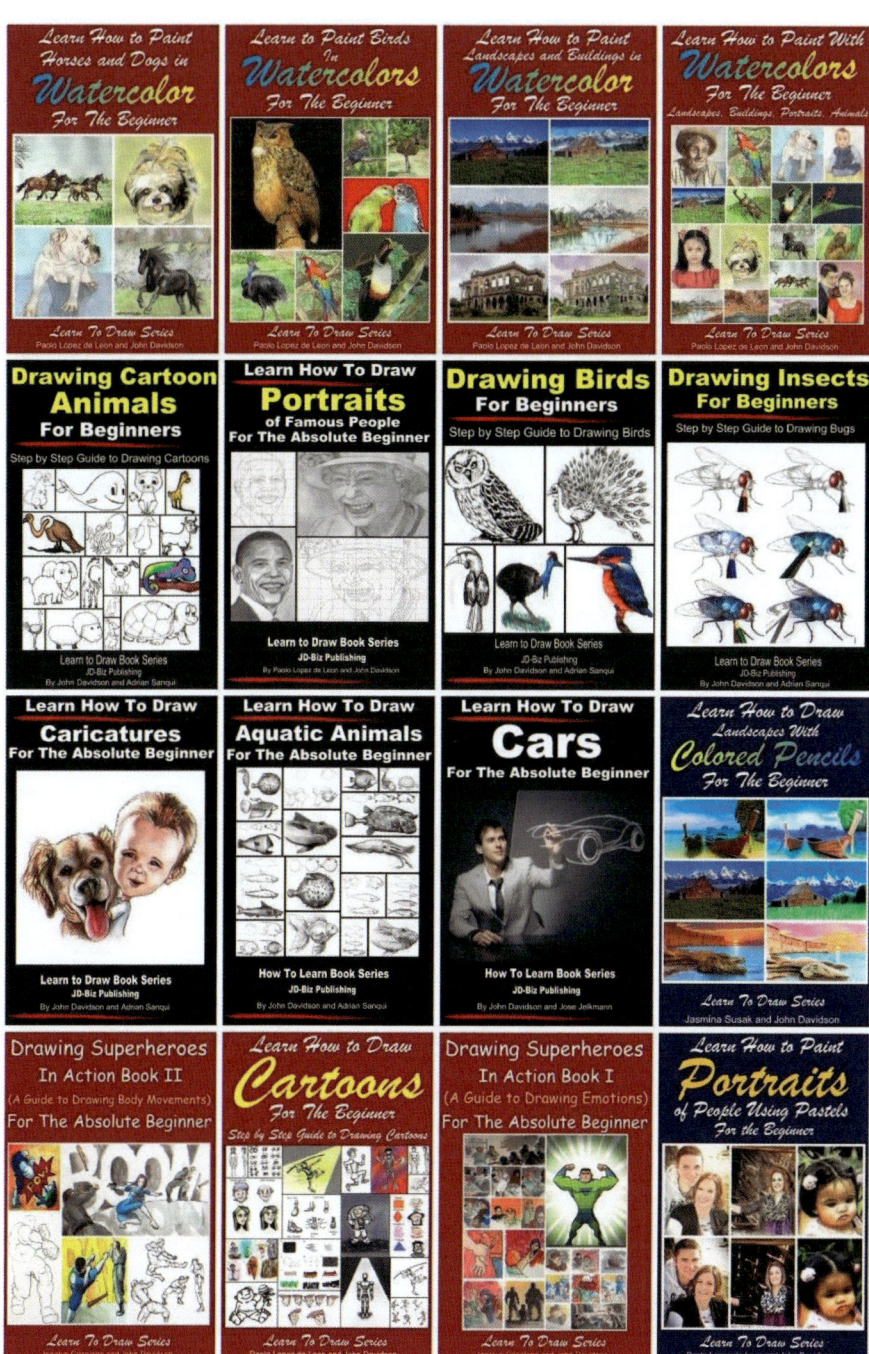

Entrepreneur Book Series

Our books are available at

1. Amazon.com

2. Barnes and Noble

3. Itunes

4. Kobo

5. Smashwords

6. Google Play Books

Download Free Books!

http://MendonCottageBooks.com

Publisher

JD-Biz Corp

P O Box 374

Mendon, Utah 84325

http://www.jd-biz.com/

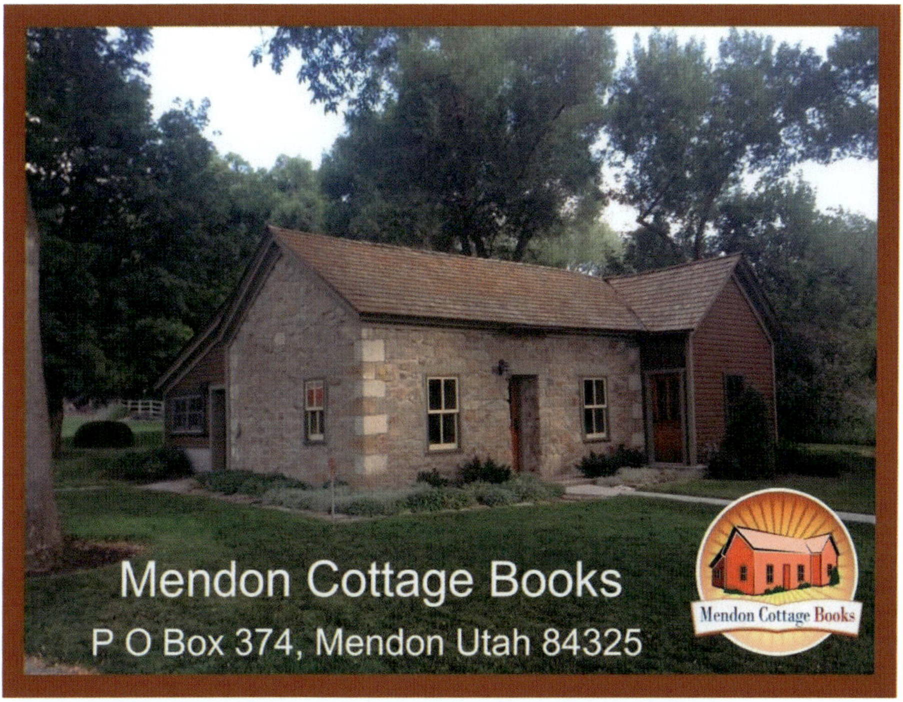

Mendon Cottage Books

P O Box 374, Mendon Utah 84325

Crock Pot Express Cookbook

Best Quick & Easy Crock Pot Express Multi Cooker Recipes

Louise Davidson

ISBN: 978-1986705004

Printed in the United States

Contents

Cooking with the Crock-Pot® Express

The very first question is whether the Crock-Pot® Express is an instant pot or a slow cooker. Well, the Crock-Pot® Express is a multipurpose appliance with eleven basic functions. It can be a steamer, rice cooker, dessert maker, yogurt maker, and soup maker. It speeds up the cooking process by a factor of 10 and uses 70 percent less energy. It is one of the top-selling kitchen appliances worldwide because of its functionality and ease of use, and it is undoubtedly a perfect addition to your kitchen. It's so versatile and convenient that you can use it whether you want to sauté, steam, pressure cook or slow cook. If you are in a hurry you can choose any of the 8 preset settings, and if you are not ready to eat right away, then you can just use the slow cooking option and come back to enjoy a delicious meal at your leisure.

Quick Starter Guide

1. The Crock-Pot® Express has a lock/unlock indicator.
2. It comes with a plastic spoon, cooking pot, steaming rack, and glass lid.
3. It has a steam release valve option.

Now let's look at the buttons—and how you can use them to cook the finest recipes!

1. Add the ingredients to the pot according to directions.
2. Secure the lid of the pot.
3. Press the function you want to use, according to the recipe.
4. Adjust temperature as per the recipe.
5. Use the time selection button to set the cooking time.
6. Rotate the steam release valve into the appropriate position for the recipe.

7. After cooking is done, press the START/STOP button.
8. Wait for 10 minutes until the steam releases.
9. Rotate the valve into the release position.
10. Open the pot, serve the meal, and enjoy.

Advantages of the Crock-Pot® Express

- The food cooked in a Crock-Pot® Express keeps all its nutrients locked in, which makes it one of the healthiest meals to enjoy.
- Slow cooking is faster than with a traditional slow cooker.
- It is very easy to clean, and all the removable parts are dishwasher-safe.
- The functions are easy to use.
- It cooks even cheap cuts of meat to tender and juicy perfection.
- It saves time and energy.
- It provides a hands-free cooking experience.

Crock Pot Express Functions and Cooking Times

Cooking Function	Default Setting	Pressure Adjustments	Temperature Adjustments	Cook Time Range
SLOW COOK	High temp / 4 h	N/A	Low-High	30 min – 20 h
STEAM	High pressure / 10 min	Low-High	N/A	3 min – 1 h
BROWN / SAUTÉ	High temp / 30 min	N/A	Low-High	5 min – 30 min
KEEP WARM	Warm temp / 4 h	N/A	Warm	30 min – 4 h
MEAT / STEW	High pressure / 35 min	Low-High	N/A	15 min – 2 h
BEANS / CHILI	High pressure / 20 min	Low-High	N/A	5 min – 2 h
RICE / RISOTTO	Low pressure / 12 min	Low-High	N/A	6 min – 30 min
YOGURT	Low temp / 8 h	N/A	Low-High	Low: 6 – 12 h High: N/A
POULTRY	High pressure / 15 min	Low-High	N/A	15 min – 2 h
DESSERT	Low pressure / 10 min	Low-High	N/A	5 min – 2 h
SOUP	High pressure / 30 min	Low-High	N/A	5 min – 2 h
MULTIGRAIN	High pressure / 40 min	Low-High	N/A	10 min – 2 h

Breakfast Recipes
Slow Cooked Cranberry Orange Steel Cut Oatmeal for Breakfast

This is a perfect bowl of oatmeal that gets its flavor from the addition of orange juice, lemon, cinnamon, and cranberries. The cranberries make this recipe a not only tasty but also much healthier breakfast treat to enjoy.

Servings: 4 – Prep Time: 8 Hours – Cook Time: 8 Hours
Pressure Level: Low

Ingredients
3 cups steel cut oats
9 cups water
1 cup cranberries, dried
Juice of 1 orange
½ teaspoon lemon zest
1 tablespoon vanilla extract
1 teaspoon cinnamon
Pinch of salt

For Topping
½ cup raw almonds, chopped

Directions
1. Dump all the listed ingredients into a Crock-Pot® Express and stir to combine.
2. Cook on the warm setting for 8 hours at low pressure.
3. Top with almonds and serve the delicious oatmeal for breakfast.

Nutrition Facts per Serving
Calories 349, total fat 10 g, carbs 53 g, protein 11 g, sodium 59 mg

Breakfast Quinoa

This is a simple breakfast recipe that provides multiple nutrients to the body.

Servings: 4 – Prep Time: 8 Hours – Cook Time: 8 Hours
Pressure Level: Low

Ingredients

3 cups quinoa, uncooked
2 cups water
½ cup brown sugar
1 teaspoon ground cinnamon
Pinch of sea salt
1 cup low-fat milk (or almond milk)
½ teaspoon vanilla bean extract
Mixed nuts (optional; serve on the side)

Directions

1. Add all the listed ingredients to a Crock-Pot® Express.
2. Stir to combine.
3. Cook on the warm setting for 8 hours at low pressure.
4. Serve with mixed nuts, if desired.

Nutrition facts per serving
Calories 564, total fat 7.7 g, carbs 103.1 g, protein 20.3 g, sodium 87 mg

Hazelnut and Chocolate Banana Bread

The richness of bananas and added nutrients from hazelnuts make this a divine breakfast meal.

Servings: 6 – Prep Time: 1 hour 20 minutes – Cook Time: 1 hour
Pressure Level: High

Ingredients
2 cups all-purpose flour
2 teaspoons baking powder
½ teaspoon baking soda
Pinch of salt
1 egg, whisked
1 cup brown sugar
1 cup yogurt
½ cup butter or coconut oil
1–2 teaspoons vanilla extract
4 ripe bananas, mashed
⅓ cup milk
¼ cup chocolate chips (dark chocolate preferred)
½ cup hazelnuts, chopped
2 cups water

Directions
1. Grease a 6-cup Bundt pan with cooking spray and line it with parchment paper.
2. In a bowl, mix the flour with the baking soda, baking powder, and salt.
3. In a separate bowl, whisk together egg, sugar, milk, yogurt, vanilla and oil. At the end, whisk in mashed bananas.
4. Combine the contents of both bowls.
5. Fold in the hazelnuts and dark chocolate chips.
6. Pour this mixture into the Bundt pan.

7. Pour 2 cups of water into the Crock-Pot® Express and place the steaming rack on top.
8. Place the Bundt pan on top of the rack.
9. Cover the pan with a piece of foil.
10. Secure the lid of the pot and seal the valve.
11. Press MULTIGRAIN.
12. Set the timer for 1 hour at high pressure.
13. Remove from pan, let cool and serve.

Nutrition Facts per Serving
Calories 576, total fat 23.4 g, carbs 83.2 g, protein 10.5 g, sodium 303 mg

Delicious Muffins for Breakfast

These muffins are cooked to perfection using a Crock-Pot®
Express; they turn out great in texture and flavor.

Servings: 4 – Prep Time: 60 minutes – Cook Time: 50 minutes
Pressure Level: High

Ingredients
Dry Ingredients
1 cup almond meal
1 cup all-purpose flour
¼ cup raw hemp seeds
1 tablespoon yeast flakes
1 teaspoon baking powder
Pinch of sea salt

Wet Ingredients
3 eggs, whisked
⅓ cup green onion, thinly sliced
1 cup cottage cheese
4 ounces Parmesan cheese, grated

Directions
1. Place a steamer rack or trivet inside a Crock-Pot®
   Express and pour in 2 cups of water.
2. In a bowl, combine all the dry ingredients.
3. In a separate bowl, whisk together all the wet ingredients.
4. Take silicone muffin cups and place muffin papers inside
   each cup.
5. Combine the contents of both bowls to make a batter.
6. Fill the silicone muffin cups with a generous amount of
   prepared batter.
7. Place the muffin cups on top of the trivet inside the pot.

8. Seal the valve, select MULTIGRAIN, and set the timer for 50 minutes at high pressure.
9. Take out the muffin cups and let cool.
10. Serve and enjoy.

Nutrition Facts per Serving
Calories 557, total fat 29.5 g, carbs 37.7 g, protein 38.4 g, sodium 598 mg

Avocado Bread

This recipe is loaded with protein, minerals, vitamins and good fat essential for growing bodies.

Servings: 6 – Prep Time: 1 hour 15 minutes – Cook Time: 1 hour
Pressure Level: High

Ingredients
4 cups all-purpose flour
¼ cup vegetable oil
1 teaspoon vanilla extract
1 cup sugar, granulated
4 organic eggs, whisked
2 teaspoons baking powder
¼ teaspoon salt
2 cups avocado, pitted and mashed
Oil spray, for greasing
Water, for pouring

Directions
1. Grease a 6-cup Bundt pan with oil spray and line it with parchment paper.
2. In a medium bowl, mix all- purpose flour, salt, sugar, and baking powder.
3. In a blender, blend avocados, eggs, oil, and vanilla extract until smooth.
4. Place the blended ingredients into the bowl.
5. Mix well.
6. Pour this mixture into the Bundt pan.
7. Place a trivet in the Crock-Pot® Express and add 2 cups of water.
8. Place the Bundt pan on top of the trivet.
9. Cover the pan with a piece of foil.
10. Secure the lid of the pot and seal the valve.

11. Press MULTIGRAIN.
12. Set the timer for 1 hour at high pressure.
13. Remove pan and let cool, then slice and serve.

Nutrition Facts per Serving
Calories 653, total fat 22 g, carbs 102.2 g, protein 13.2 g, sodium 144 mg

Oatmeal with Berries

The hit combination of berries and oatmeal makes this a delicious breakfast to enjoy.

Servings: 6 – Prep Time: 20 minutes – Cook Time: 12 minutes
Pressure Level: High

Ingredients
1 cup steel cut oats
3 cups water
2 tablespoons coconut oil
Dash of Sea salt
2 teaspoons brown sugar

Topping:
½ cup strawberries, chopped
½ cup blueberries, washed

Directions
1. Combine all of the listed ingredients in a Crock-Pot® Express.
2. Press the MULTIGRAIN button and set pressure to high.
3. Adjust the timer to 12 minutes. The steam release valve should be closed and sealed.
4. Serve it with strawberries and blueberries topping.
5. Enjoy.

Nutrition Facts per Serving
Calories 105, total fat 5.5 g, carbs 12.9 g, protein 2 g, sodium 32 mg

Chicken & Poultry Recipes

Coconut Chicken Curry

This rich and tasteful coconut curry goes well with boiled rice and can be enjoyed at dinner or at lunch.

Servings: 4 – Prep Time: 60 minutes – Cook Time: 45 minutes
Pressure Level: Low

Ingredients
2 pounds chicken, skinless and boneless
Salt, to taste
⅓ teaspoon fresh-ground black pepper
2 tablespoons canola or other vegetable oil
2 white onions, sliced
1 zucchini, peeled and sliced
4 cloves of garlic, minced
1 teaspoon minced ginger root
1 cup coconut milk
3 teaspoons Thai green curry paste

Garnishing and Side Servings
2 tablespoons lemon juice
1 teaspoon soy sauce
2 cups jasmine rice, cooked

Directions
1. Cook the rice according to package instructions.
2. Preheat the Crock-Pot® Express by turning on the sauté mode at high temperature.
3. Season the chicken with salt and black pepper.
4. Heat half of the oil in the Crock-Pot® Express and sauté onions in it.
5. Add chicken and let it cook for 7 minutes.

6. Transfer the chicken to a separate plate.
7. Add the remaining oil to the Crock-Pot® Express and then add the zucchini, ginger, curry paste, and garlic.
8. Stir for 5 minutes, and then add the coconut milk.
9. Press the START/STOP button and add the chicken mixture to the pot.
10. Secure the lid of the Crock-Pot® Express and open the steam release valve.
11. Press the SLOW COOK button and cook the chicken for 30 minutes at low pressure
12. Serve it drizzled with lemon juice and soy sauce.
13. Enjoy over cooked rice.

Nutrition Facts per Serving
Calories 812, total fat 30 g, carbs 72 g, protein 60.8 g, sodium 1240 mg

Spicy Turkey Recipe

This recipe gets all its spiciness from the addition of red chilies and paprika.

Servings: 3 – Prep Time: 50 minutes – Cook Time: 40 minutes
Pressure Level: Low-Marinating time: 2 hours

Ingredients for Rub
¼ cup brown sugar
2 tablespoons paprika
2 tablespoons chili powder
Salt, to taste
2 teaspoons garlic powder
1 teaspoon ginger paste
2 pounds turkey pieces
1 cup nonfat yogurt
1 cup onions, chopped
2 tablespoons olive oil
½ cup soy sauce

Directions
1. In a bowl, combine brown sugar, paprika, chili powder, salt, garlic powder, ginger, and yogurt.
2. Rub the mixture over the turkey pieces and refrigerate for a few hours to marinate.
3. Turn on the sauté mode of the Crock-Pot® Express and add onion and oil. Cook until brown.
4. Add the marinated turkey and cook for another 4 minutes.
5. Add the soy sauce and press the START/STOP button.
6. Secure the lid of the Crock-Pot® Express and open the steam release valve.
7. Select the SLOW COOK button and cook for 30 minutes at low pressure.
8. Serve and enjoy with cooked rice.

Nutrition Facts per Serving
Calories 773, total fat 27 g, carbs 31.4 g, protein 98 g, sodium 2773 mg

Chicken Provencal

Olives and capsicum make this chicken taste great, and they also load the recipe with healthy nutrients like fiber, vitamins, protein, mineral, and magnesium.

Servings: 4 – Prep Time: 50 minutes – Cook Time: 40 minutes
Pressure Level: High

Ingredients
1 teaspoon olive oil
6 cloves garlic, crushed
1 onion, sliced
2 green bell peppers, deseeded, sliced
⅓ cup white wine
2 cups tomatoes, chopped
1 cup olives, pitted and chopped
1½ pounds chicken thigh fillets, skinless
2 anchovies
Salt and fresh-ground black pepper, to taste

Directions
1. Press the BROWN/SAUTÉ button of the Crock-Pot® Express and set the temperature to high.
2. Press the START/STOP button and add the oil.
3. Preheat it for a few minutes and then add the garlic, onion, and bell peppers.
4. Cook for 5 minutes.
5. Add the wine and cook it until reduced to half.
6. Press the START/STOP button and add the remaining ingredients one by one.
7. Lock the lid and press POULTRY.
8. Set timer for 30 minutes at high pressure.
9. Serve hot.

Nutrition Facts per Serving
Calories 1046, total fat 45 g, carbs 14 g, protein 148 g, sodium 1325 mg

Duck Ragu

This is a very simple, delicious, and hearty recipe to enjoy.

Servings: 4 – Prep Time: 45 minutes – Cook Time: 35 minutes
Pressure Level: High

Ingredients
2 tablespoons butter
1 pound duck breasts, skin on
4 ounces bacon, chopped
3 cloves garlic, crushed
2 onions, finely chopped
½ teaspoon bay leaf, crumbled
2 tablespoons tomato paste
½ cup red wine
1 cup button mushrooms, sliced
Salt and black pepper, to taste
2 cups cooked pasta (for serving)
4 ounces Parmesan cheese

Directions
1. Press the BROWN/SAUTÉ button of the Crock-Pot® Express and set the temperature to high.
2. Press the START/STOP button to start the cooking.
3. Add the butter to the pot and cook for 1 minute.
4. Add the duck meat and let it cook for 4 minutes.
5. Once brown, remove it from the pot.
6. Add the bacon, garlic, onion, and bay leaf to the pot and sauté for a few minutes
7. Add the tomato paste and cook for a few minutes.
8. Add the wine and cook until reduced to half.
9. Add the mushrooms.
10. Adjust seasoning by adding salt and pepper.
11. Press the START/STOP button.

12. Lock the Crock-Pot® Express lid and press the POULTRY button.
13. Set pressure to high and cook for 20 minutes. Make sure the steam release valve is in the closed position.
14. Serve over cooked pasta, sprinkled with Parmesan cheese if desired.

Nutrition Facts per Serving
Calories 589, total fat 28 g, carbs 30 g, protein 48 g, sodium 969 mg

Steamed Chicken

This is a very simple recipe which uses the Crock-Pot® Express to steam the chicken to perfection.

Servings: 2 – Prep Time: 20 minutes – Cook Time: 10 minutes
Pressure Level: High

Ingredients
2 green onions, chopped
4 cloves garlic, minced
1 tablespoon soy sauce
2 tablespoons lemon juice
1 tablespoon fish sauce
1 teaspoon olive oil
1 teaspoon ginger, grated
6 chicken breasts, skinless
Salt, to taste
Black pepper, to taste
2 tablespoons sesame seeds, for topping
2 cups water, for pouring

Directions
1. In a large bowl, combine onions, salt, black pepper, garlic, oil, fish sauce, lemon juice, soy sauce, and ginger. Mix well.
2. Coat the chicken breasts with the bowl mixture.
3. Place a baking sheet onto an 8×8 square pan.
4. Layer the chicken pieces into the pan.
5. Drizzle the remaining sauce on top.
6. Bring the corners of the baking sheet to the center in order to form a shape like a parcel.
7. Pour water into the Crock-Pot® Express.
8. Place the trivet inside.

9. Adjust the chicken parcels on top of the trivet.
10. Lock the lid of the Crock-Pot® Express and set the pressure to high.
11. Press the STEAM button and set the timer 10 minutes.
12. Afterward, quick release the steam.
13. Remove the chicken parcels and serve with a sprinkle of sesame seeds on top.
14. Enjoy.

Nutrition Facts per Serving
Calories 509, total fat 21.3 g, carbs 9 g, protein 65.6 g, sodium 2600 mg

Coq Au Vin

This recipe combines several rich and flavorful vegetables on one plate to give you mouthwatering taste.

Servings: 8 – Prep Time: 35 minutes – Cook Time: 25 minutes
Pressure Level: High

Ingredients
2 leeks, halved
2 sprigs fresh parsley
1 teaspoon bay leaf
2 tablespoons olive oil
3 pounds chicken thighs, fat removed
¼ cup butter
8 ounces bacon, chopped
5 ounces button mushrooms, chopped
6 shallots, sliced
4 cloves garlic, crushed
⅓ cup flour
½ cup tomato paste
2 carrots, peeled, diced
2½ cups red wine
1 cup chicken stock
Salt and black ground pepper, to taste

Directions
1. Press the BROWN/SAUTÉ button of the Crock-Pot® Express and add oil.
2. Preheat for 2 minutes, then press the START/STOP button.
3. Add the chicken to the pot and cook it until brown.
4. Add butter and bacon to the pot and cook it until crispy.
5. Add the mushrooms, leeks, garlic and all the remaining ingredients except the flour and tomato paste.

6. Cook for 8 minutes, until tender.
7. Stir in flour and tomato paste.
8. Secure the lid of the Crock-Pot® Express.
9. Press the POULTRY button and set the timer to 10 minutes at high pressure. The steam release valve should be closed.
10. Serve hot.

Nutrition Facts per Serving
Calories 684, total fat 34 g, carbs 16 g, protein 62.5 g, sodium 994 mg

Chicken Wings

These wings are marinated to perfection in sweet and spicy sauces.

Servings: 6 – Prep Time: 22 minutes – Cook Time: 15 minutes
Pressure Level: High-Marinating time: 2 hours

Ingredients
4 pounds chicken wings
1 cup soy sauce
½ cup honey
2 teaspoons ground ginger
2 teaspoons garlic powder
Salt to taste
Black pepper, to taste

Directions
1. Combine all the listed ingredients in a bowl and let sit in the refrigerator for a few hours.
2. Dump all the ingredients into the Crock-Pot® Express and secure the lid.
3. Press the POULTRY button and set the timer to 15 minutes at high pressure. The steam release valve should be closed.
4. Serve hot.

Nutrition Facts per Serving
Calories 688, total fat 66 g, carbs 60 g, protein 63 g, sodium 3392 mg

Chicken Breast with Gravy

A very richly flavored dish that is prepared in just a few minutes with the help of the Crock-Pot® Express.

Servings: 4 – Prep Time: 30 minutes – Cook Time: 22 minutes
Pressure Level: High

Ingredients

2 pounds chicken breast, butterfly cut
Salt, to taste
Black pepper, to taste
¼ cup onion gravy mix
⅓ cup almond flour, for dredging
1 cup mushrooms, chopped
1 cup water
2 tablespoons olive oil

Directions

1. Mix the almond flour, salt, black pepper, and onion gravy mix together in a large bowl.
2. Dredge the breast pieces in the flour mixture.
3. Turn on the sauté mode of the Crock-Pot® Express, add the oil and cook for 1 minute.
4. Add the mushrooms and cook for 1 minute.
5. Add water to the pot.
6. Add the chicken breasts to the pot along with bowl mixture.
7. Press the POULTRY button and set the timer for 20 minutes at high pressure.
8. Serve breast pieces with gravy from the pot.
9. Enjoy.

Nutrition Facts per Serving
Calories 366, total fat 13.8 g, carbs 7 g, protein 49 g, sodium 678 mg

Fish & Seafood Recipes

Steamed Shrimp

The Crock-Pot® Express lets you prepare delicious shrimp in delicious gravy in just 3 minutes! This is a very delicious, mouthwatering, low calorie, light and flavorful seafood recipe to serve as lunch or dinner.

Servings: 2 – Prep Time: 5 minutes – Cook Time: 3 minutes
Pressure Level: High

Ingredients
1 pound shrimp, tail on, deveined and peeled
1 cup parsley, chopped
2 tablespoons vegetable or olive oil
3 tablespoons red wine vinegar
4 cloves garlic, minced
⅓ teaspoon salt
½ teaspoon black pepper
Hot pepper flakes, to taste
1 cup water

Directions
1. Add water to the Crock-Pot® Express and then place the steaming rack inside the pot.
2. Add the shrimp and press the STEAM button.
3. Set the pressure to high.
4. Adjust time to 3 minutes.
5. In a food processor, finely chop all the remaining ingredients.
6. Transfer the blended ingredients to the pot.
7. Serve shrimp with blended ingredients.
8. Enjoy.

Nutrition Facts per Serving
Calories 415, total fat 18 g, carbs 8 g, protein 53 g, sodium 966 mg

Salmon Parcels

Prepared in a unique way, but one of the best salmon recipes around! This recipe is rich in flavor and filled with the goodness of omega-3s.

Servings: 2 – Prep Time: 10 minutes – Cook Time: 3 minutes
Pressure Level: High

Ingredients
4 8-ounce salmon fillets
½ lemon, finely sliced
½ cup fresh basil
⅓ cup fresh dill
¼ cup butter, room temperature
Salt and black pepper
2 cups water, for pouring

Directions
1. Place the salmon in the middle of an 8×8 inch baking paper.
2. Sprinkle the basil, butter, lemon, and dill over the salmon and bring the corners of the baking paper to the center to form a parcel.
3. Pour two cups of water into the Crock-Pot® Express.
4. Place the steaming rack on top.
5. Adjust the parcel over the rack.
6. Press the STEAM button and set the pressure to high.
7. Set the timer for 3 minutes.
8. Serve sprinkled with salt and pepper.

Nutrition Facts per Serving
Calories 701, total fat 45, carbs 6 g, protein 71.3 g, sodium 345 mg

Express Paella

Here is another classic hit recipe to enjoy using shrimp, rice, and vegetables.

Servings: 6 – Prep Time: 25 minutes – Cook Time: 18 minutes
Pressure Level: Low

Ingredients
2 teaspoons olive oil
1 pound chorizo, sliced
4 cloves garlic, crushed
2 onions, chopped
2 red bell peppers, seeds removed
2 cups chicken stock
½ cup whole green peas
1 cup long grain rice
1 teaspoon sugar
2 pounds shrimp, peeled, deveined
14 ounces tomatoes, chopped
Salt and black pepper, to taste

Directions
1. Turn on the sauté mode of the pot and set the temperature to high.
2. Add oil and chorizo and cook for 2 minutes.
3. Once brown, remove from pot.
4. Add garlic, onion, and bell peppers to the pot and cook for 5 minutes until tender.
5. Press the START/STOP button and add the remaining ingredients.
6. Close the lid, press the RICE/RISOTTO button, and set the time to 10 minutes at low pressure.
7. Once cooking is complete, quick release the steam.
8. Adjust seasoning and serve with cooked chorizo.
9. Enjoy.

Nutrition Facts per Serving
Calories 651, total fat 32 g, carbs 39 g, protein 46 g, sodium 1596 mg

Divine Salmon

This is a very healthy, mouthwatering, rich and garlicky recipe to enjoy.

Servings: 4 – Prep Time: 20 minutes – Cook Time: 15 minutes
Pressure Level: High-Marinating time: 20 minutes

Ingredients
4 7-ounce salmon fillets
6 cloves garlic, minced
2 tablespoons ginger, grated
2 tablespoons brown sugar
1 teaspoon sesame seeds
1 tablespoon corn starch + 2 tablespoons water
⅓ cup soy sauce
½ cup water
½ cup sherry
¼ cup sesame oil

Directions
1. To a small bowl, add soy sauce, water, oil, seeds, sherry, garlic, ginger, and sugar.
2. Place salmon in a loaf pan.
3. Pour half of the mixture on top of the salmon.
4. Marinate salmon for 20 minutes.
5. Place trivet inside the Crock-Pot® Express and pour water into the pot.
6. Place the pan on the trivet.
7. Cook on high pressure for 10 minutes.
8. Meanwhile, heat the reserved sauce in a separate saucepan.
9. Add the cornstarch mixture to the pan.
10. Once thickened, set aside.
11. Open the pot and then quick release steam.
12. Pour the saucepan mixture over the cooked fish.
13. Serve and enjoy.

Nutrition Facts per Serving
Calories 419, total fat 25 g, carbs 11 g, protein 36.5 g, sodium 1280 mg

Coconut Gravy with Seafood

The addition of coconut milk makes this a creamy and rich tasting dish to enjoy.

Servings: 6 – Prep Time: 13 minutes – Cook Time: 7 minutes
Pressure Level: High

Ingredients
2 tablespoons coconut oil
½ tablespoon garlic, minced
Zest of 1 lemon
4 cups shrimp, washed
3 tablespoons fish sauce
Black pepper, to taste
Salt, to taste
4 large onions
1 red chili, sliced
3 cups coconut milk
1 1-inch piece galangal or ginger
1 cup lemongrass, cut into pieces

Directions
1. Turn on the sauté mode of the Crock-Pot® Express and add oil and onions.
2. Cook for a few minutes and then add garlic, red chili, lemongrass, galangal, shrimp, fish sauce, salt, and pepper.
3. Set the timer for 5 minutes at high pressure.
4. After 5 minutes, release the steam valve and press the BROWN/SAUTÉ button.
5. Add the milk and lemon zest.
6. Let simmer for 2 minutes.
7. Just before serving the dish, remove lemongrass stick and galangal.
8. Serve and enjoy.

Nutrition Facts per Serving
Calories 715, total fat 31.1 g, carbs 28 g, protein 88 g, sodium 1305 mg

Honey-Glazed Shrimps

This is a very sweet seafood dish that gives your taste buds a roller coaster ride of hearty flavors.

Servings: 4 – Prep Time: 15 minutes – Cook Time: 11 minutes
Pressure Level: High

Ingredients
¼ cup sesame oil
½ pound green beans
3 pounds shrimp
Salt, to taste
Pepper, to taste
½ cup orange juice
2 teaspoons honey
2 teaspoons rice wine vinegar
4 teaspoons toasted sesame seeds

Directions
1. Turn on the sauté mode of the Crock-Pot® Express and add oil.
2. Add the salt, pepper and green beans.
3. Cook until soft.
4. Add the juice, honey, rice wine and vinegar.
5. Cook for 5 minutes.
6. Now add the shrimp, press the STEAM button, and set the pressure to high.
7. Set the timer for 4 minutes.
8. Serve with a sprinkle of sesame seeds.

Nutrition Facts per Serving
Calories 586, total fat 21 g, carbs 16 g, protein 76 g, sodium 873 mg

Pork and Lamb Recipes

Lamb Shanks with Lemon

This is a very spicy and tangy recipe. You can replace the wheat flour with almond flour if preferred.

Servings: 6 – Prep Time: 50 minutes – Cook Time: 40 minutes
Pressure Level: High

Ingredients
6 lamb shanks
½ cup flour
½ cup olive oil
3 cloves garlic, crushed
4 onions, chopped
1 cup chicken stock
2 fresh dill sprigs
1 lemon, zest
2 tablespoons lemon juice
Black pepper, to taste
Salt, to taste

Directions
1. Dust the lamb shanks with the flour.
2. Now press the SAUTÉ button of the Crock-Pot® Express and add onions and oil.
3. Sauté the onions until brown, and then add garlic and lamb.
4. Cook the lamb until brown.
5. Remove lamb.
6. Add all the remaining ingredients to the Crock-Pot® Express.
7. Cook for few minutes.
8. Add the lamb shanks.

9. Press the START/STOP button.
10. Secure the lid and press the MEAT/STEW button.
11. Press the START/STOP button and let cook for 30 minutes at high pressure.
12. Serve and enjoy.

Nutrition Facts per Serving
Calories 648, total fat 33 g, carbs 16.6 g, protein 69 g, sodium 317 mg

Pulled Pork

This is a tender, juicy and aromatic recipe that includes tons of spices that make it a divine mouthwatering treat to enjoy.

Servings: 6 – Prep Time: 3 hours – Cook Time: 2 hours 10 minutes
Pressure Level: High

Ingredients

2 tablespoons chili powder
Salt flakes, to taste
1 teaspoon brown sugar
1 teaspoon ground cumin
⅓ teaspoon cayenne
⅓ teaspoon turmeric
1 teaspoon dry oregano, or to taste
1 teaspoon onion powder
1 teaspoon garlic powder
½ teaspoon cinnamon
⅓ teaspoon ground cloves
2 tablespoons vegetable oil
2 leeks, sliced
3 pounds pork shoulder, boneless
1 pound tomatoes, chopped
½ cup water
2 teaspoons apple cider vinegar
Salt and black pepper, to taste

To Serve (Side Servings)
6 soft tacos, or as needed
⅓ cup guacamole, or as needed
1 cup sour cream, to serve

Directions

1. Combine all of the listed ingredients (except the oil, tomatoes, vinegar, and water) in a bowl and rub the pork well with the mixture.
2. Let it sit for a few minutes before starting the cooking process.
3. Add oil to the Crock-Pot® Express and press the BROWN/SAUTÉ button.
4. Set the temperature to high.
5. Start the Crock-Pot® Express and add the contents of the bowl to the pot.
6. Let cook for 5–8 minutes and then add tomatoes, water, and apple cider vinegar.
7. Secure the lid and press the MEAT/STEW button.
8. Cook on high pressure for 2 hours.
9. Serve with side servings.

Nutrition Facts per Serving
Calories 1013, total fat 68 g, carbs 38.7 g, protein 60.4 g, sodium 725 mg

Double-Smoked Bacon & Leeks

This is a very classic recipe which is rich in intense flavors.

Servings: 6 – Prep Time: 4 hours – Cook Time: 3 hours 15 minutes
Pressure Level: Low

Ingredients
6 double-smoked bacon slices, chopped
4 leeks, chopped
2 onions, chopped
2 jalapeno peppers, chopped
4 cloves garlic, minced
1 tablespoon fresh thyme, chopped
1 teaspoon ground cumin
2 teaspoons Cajun seasoning blend
1 cup white beans, drained and rinsed
1 cup chickpeas, drained and rinsed
1 can kidney beans, drained and rinsed
1 cup black beans, drained
4 teaspoons all-purpose flour
4 cups chicken broth
1 cup whipping cream
1 cup cheddar cheese, shredded

Directions
1. Press the SAUTÉ button of the Crock-Pot® Express and let it preheat.
2. Add bacon to the pot and cook until lightly brown.
3. Drain the half of the bacon fat from the pot.
4. Add onions and cook until brown.
5. Add leeks, garlic, jalapeno, thyme, and cumin.
6. Stir well and season with Cajun seasoning blend.
7. Let cook for 5 minutes.

8. Add the white beans, black beans, chickpeas and kidney beans.
9. Sprinkle the flour over the beans.
10. Cook for a few minutes and then add the broth.
11. Press the SLOW COOK button and let cook for 3 hours at low pressure. Make sure the steam valve is open.
12. After 3 hours press the START/STOP button.
13. Open the pot and add cream.
14. Stir in cheese.
15. Serve with bread.

Nutrition Facts per Serving
Calories 699, total fat 19.3 g, carbs 95 g, protein 39 g, sodium 897 mg

Slow-Cooker Pork Chops

These pork chops are slow cooked with creamy mushroom soup for 2 hours, making them creamy and tender.

Servings: 3 – Prep Time: 2 hours – Cook Time: 2 hours
Pressure Level: Low

Ingredients
6 pork loin chops
⅓ teaspoon black pepper
4 cloves garlic, finely chopped
1 cup creamy mushroom soup
¼ cup cornstarch
¼ cup water

Directions
1. Combine all the ingredients in the Crock-Pot® Express and press the SLOW COOK button.
2. Start the pot and let it cook for 2 hours at low pressure.
3. Serve and enjoy.

Nutrition Facts per Serving
Calories 594, total fat 41 g, carbs 16 g, protein 37.3 g, sodium 377 mg

Pork and Squash Ragout

This is a very healthy pork dish prepared with butternut squash.

Servings: 6 – Prep Time: 2 hours – Cook Time: 2 hours
Pressure Level: High

Ingredients

3 pounds boneless pork , chopped

2 cups tomatoes, diced

1 cup red kidney beans, drained

1 cup butternut squash, peeled and cubed

2 cups onions, chopped

½ cup green bell peppers

1 teaspoon minced garlic

Salt and pepper, to taste

Directions

1. Combine all the ingredients in the Crock-Pot® Express and press the SLOW COOK button.
2. Press the START/STOP button and set the pressure to high for 2 hours.
3. Serve the dish.

Nutrition Facts per Serving
Calories 582, total fat 15.7 g, carbs 28.4 g, protein 78 g, sodium 136 mg

Slow Cook Pork Stew

Another hit recipe that can be devoured with boiled rice or couscous and boiled eggs. In fact, any side serving can go really well with this recipe!

Servings: 6 – Prep Time: 2 hours – Cook Time: 2 hours
Pressure Level: High

Ingredients
Main Ingredients
2 pounds boneless pork, cubed
1 cup beef broth
1 cup white onions
1 cup tomatoes, chopped
1 teaspoon garlic, minced
1 teaspoon ginger root, grated
⅓ teaspoon ground cinnamon
½ teaspoon ground turmeric
Salt, to taste
Black pepper, to taste
1 bay leaf

Garnishing Ingredients
1 cup raisins
½ cup whole almonds, toasted
4 hard-boiled eggs, chopped
2–4 cups couscous, side servings

Directions
1. Combine all the main ingredients in a Crock-Pot® Express.
2. Press the SLOW COOK button and start the pot.
3. Set the timer for 2 hours at high pressure.
4. After 2 hours, press the START/STOP button.

5. Release the steam and open the pot.
6. Discard the bay leaf.
7. Serve over cooked couscous with a garnish of egg, raisins, and almonds.
8. Enjoy.

Nutrition Facts per Serving
Calories 615, total fat 13 g, carbs 69 g, protein 54.4 g, sodium 293 mg

Slow Cook Country-Style Pork Ribs

No dipping sauce is needed while enjoying these pork ribs, as the flavor are intense and the plum sauce makes it a mouth-watering treat all by itself.

Servings: 4 – Prep Time: 2 hours – Cook Time: 2 hours
Pressure Level: High

Ingredients
3 pounds country-style pork ribs
10 ounces plum sauce
⅓ cup honey
2 tablespoons soy sauce
2 tablespoons cornstarch +1 tablespoon water
⅓ cup orange juice
Salt and pepper, to taste

Directions
1. Grease the bottom of the Crock-Pot® Express with cooking spray.
2. Layer the ribs into the pot and then add honey, plum sauce, soy sauce, and orange juice.
3. Press the SLOW COOK button.
4. Press the START/STOP button to start cooking.
5. Set the timer for 2 hours at high pressure.
6. Once the timer beeps, release the steam and press the START/STOP button to stop cooking.
7. Open the pot and add the cornstarch mixture.
8. Turn on the sauté mode and let simmer for 2 minutes.
9. Sprinkle in salt and black pepper.
10. Once thickened, serve and enjoy.

Nutrition Facts per Serving
Calories 691, total fat 12.5 g, carbs 53 g, protein 91 g, sodium 647 mg

Slow Cooked Pork with Prunes

This is a simple, easy and mouthwatering recipe to enjoy.

Servings: 10 – Prep Time: 2 hours – Cook Time: 2 hours
Pressure Level: High

Ingredients

Main Ingredients

3 pounds boneless pork loin

12 ounces prunes, pitted

3 cups chicken broth

1 teaspoon lemon zest

2 teaspoons lemon juice

Salt and black pepper, to taste

Side Servings

6 cups couscous, warm and cooked

Directions

1. Combine all main ingredients in the Crock-Pot® Express.
2. Press the SLOW COOK button and set the timer to 2 hours at high pressure.
3. Serve the cooked pork with prunes over couscous.
4. Enjoy.

Nutrition Facts per Serving
Calories 678, total fat 6 g, carbs 102.4 g, protein 51 g, sodium 318 mg

Beef Recipes

Delicious Beef Stew

The combination of vegetables goes well with the beef, making this recipe a hit with everybody.

Servings: 6 – Prep Time: 3 hours – Cook Time: 2 hours 25 minutes
Pressure Level: High

Ingredients
2 teaspoons olive oil
2 pounds stewing beef
Salt and pepper, to taste
4 cloves garlic, minced
2 teaspoons fresh thyme, chopped
¼ cup tomato paste
1½ cups carrots, diced
3 cups baby potatoes, cubed
1½ cups pearl onions, chopped
½ cup red wine
3 cups beef broth
1 bay leaf
3 tablespoons all-purpose flour
½ cup peas, thawed
2 tablespoons chives, chopped

Directions
1. Turn on the sauté mode of the pot and set pressure to high.
2. Add oil and then dump in the beef.
3. Sprinkle salt and pepper over the meat.
4. Cook while stirring for 5 minutes.
5. Add the remaining ingredients one by one, excluding the flour.

6. Press the START/STOP button and secure the lid of the pot.
7. Select the SLOW COOK button and cook for 2 hours at high pressure.
8. Press the START/STOP button and release the steam.
9. Take a small bowl and whisk the flour with ½ cup of liquid from the pot.
10. Pour the flour mixture into the Crock-Pot® Express.
11. Slow cook for 20 minutes at high pressure.
12. Remove bay leaf and serve.

Nutrition Facts per Serving
Calories 404, total fat 11.9 g, carbs 17.1 g, protein 51.4 g, sodium 511 mg

Beef with Cauliflower

This is a unique and versatile dish whose flavor is enhanced by the addition of cauliflower.

Servings: 6 – Prep Time: 2 hours 20 minutes – Cook Time: 2 hours
Pressure Level: High

Ingredients
4 pounds beef, boneless, lean, and chopped
1 cup beef broth
1 cup red onion, chopped
2 tablespoons olive oil
4 cloves garlic, minced
2 teaspoons ginger root, minced
½ teaspoon turmeric, ground
½ teaspoon cumin
Salt and black pepper, to taste
2 cups cauliflower florets, cubed
4 eggs, boiled and chopped (for garnish)

Directions
1. Turn on the sauté mode of the Crock-Pot® Express and add oil and onions.
2. Cook for 2 minutes, until brown.
3. Add beef, ginger, and garlic.
4. Let cook for 5 minutes and then add turmeric, cumin, salt, and pepper.
5. Pour in the broth.
6. Secure the lid and press the SLOW COOK button.
7. Set the timer for 2 hours at high temperature.
8. Afterward, release the steam and open the pot.
9. Add the cauliflower florets and press the STEAM button.
10. Cook for 10 minutes and open the pot after releasing the steam.

11. The meat should be tender by now.
12. The delicious stew is ready.
13. Serve it with cooked eggs.

Nutrition Facts per Serving
Calories 671, total fat 26.8 g, carbs 4.9 g, protein 98 g, sodium 379 mg

Beef & Mushroom Recipe

This is a very healthy, hearty and aromatic dish that leaves you fully satisfied by making you feel fuller for longer .

Servings: 6 – Prep Time: 5 hours – Cook Time: 4 hours 10 minutes
Pressure Level: low

Ingredients
2 tablespoons vegetable oil
1 pound cremini mushroom, sliced
1 white onion, sliced
2 pounds beef sirloin steak, cut into bite-size slices
Salt and pepper, to taste
4 cloves garlic, minced
1 tablespoon paprika
½ cup tomato paste
2 cups low-sodium beef broth
1 teaspoon all-purpose flour
2 tablespoons Worcestershire sauce
1 cup parsley, chopped fresh
14 ounces egg noodles, cooked

Directions
1. Press the BROWN/SAUTÉ button on the pot and set the temperature to high.
2. Press the START/STOP button.
3. Allow the pot to preheat.
4. Add the oil along with the onions, mushrooms, and beef.
5. Cook for 5 minutes.
6. Add salt, pepper and tomato paste.
7. Cook for one minute.
8. Add garlic and paprika, broth, and Worcestershire sauce.
9. Take some liquid from the pot and mix it with the flour.
10. Add the flour mixture to the pot.

11. Press the START/STOP button.
12. Secure the lid and select slow cook at low temperature for 4 hours.
13. Press START/STOP and let cook for 4 hours.
14. Serve the cooked mixture over egg noodles.
15. Enjoy with a garnish of parsley.

Nutrition Facts per Serving
Calories 360, total fat 7 g, carbs 30 g, protein 43 g, sodium 872 mg

Meaty Stuffed Peppers

The pepper is stuffed with meaty goodness that results in a rich flavor.

Servings: 4 – Prep Time: 25 minutes – Cook Time: 15 minutes
Pressure Level: High

Ingredients
6 bell peppers, center cored (any color)
1½ pounds ground beef
2-ounce can of black beans, drained and rinsed
3 cups Pepper Jack cheese, shredded
2 cups corn, drained
2 white onions, diced
3 diced tomatoes, chopped
8-ounce can of enchilada sauce
½ cup white wine
1 teaspoon cumin
1 teaspoon garlic powder
Salt and black pepper, to taste
3 tablespoons olive oil

Directions
1. Center core the bell peppers and then set aside.
2. Turn on the sauté mode of the pot.
3. Set temperature to high.
4. Add the oil to the pot and brown the beef in it for a few minutes.
5. Press the START/STOP button.
6. Stir in the black beans, cheese, salt, tomatoes, onion, corn, enchilada sauce, garlic powder, and cumin.
7. Stir well.
8. Fill the center of the bell peppers with the mixture.
9. Place a rack in the pot and then pour in two cups of water.

10. Place the stuffed bell peppers on top of the rack.
11. Secure the lid of the pot and press the BEANS/CHILI button.
12. Set the temperature to low.
13. Set the timer for 15 minutes at high pressure.
14. Press the START/STOP button.
15. Serve and enjoy.

Nutrition Facts per Serving
Calories 472, total fat 16.2 g, carbs 25 g, protein 53 g, sodium 425 mg

Spiced Ground Beef with Potato

The addition of garam masala powder makes this a savory and spicy dish bursting with flavors.

Servings: 6 – Prep Time: 75 minutes – Cook Time: 65 minutes
Pressure Level: High

Ingredients
2 cups potatoes, peeled and cubed
2 pounds ground beef
1 cup white onion, chopped
1 cup tomato
1 teaspoon ginger paste
1 teaspoon garlic paste
½ teaspoon turmeric
½ teaspoon red chili
1 teaspoon garam masala
¼ cup olive oil
⅓ cup water

Directions
1. Press the BROWN/SAUTÉ button of the Crock-Pot® Express and set the temperature and pressure to high.
2. Press the START/STOP button.
3. Allow the pot to preheat.
4. Add the oil and onions and cook for 2 minutes.
5. Add the tomatoes, ginger and garlic paste.
6. Let cook or 4 minutes.
7. Add the ground beef and let it cook until browned.
8. Add all the spices and stir few times.
9. Once the meat turns brown, add the potatoes and water.
10. Stir and turn off the sauté mode.
11. Press the START/STOP button.
12. Press the SLOW COOK button and set for 50 minutes at high pressure.
13. Serve and enjoy.

Nutrition Facts per Serving
Calories 346, total fat 13 g, carbs 33 g, protein 24 g, sodium 525 mg

Corned Beef (Pressure Cooked)

This is a simple and classic recipe to enjoy at dinner or lunch time. The recipe is full of healthy ingredients that make it a complete meal.

Servings: 4 – Prep Time: 55 minutes – Cook Time: 35minutes
Pressure Level: High

Ingredients

2-pound packet of corned beef brisket with seasoning
4 red potatoes, cut into chunks
1 pound baby carrots, chopped and peeled
1 head of cabbage, sliced
2 cloves garlic, minced
2 tablespoons sugar
2 tablespoons apple cider vinegar
Salt and black pepper, to taste

Directions

1. Place the potatoes, cabbage, and carrots into the Crock-Pot® Express.
2. Add the garlic, sugar, apple cider vinegar, salt, and black pepper on top of the vegetables.
3. Rub the packet seasoning on the beef and place it inside the pot.
4. Secure the lid of the Crock-Pot® Express.
5. Press the MEAT/STEW button and set the timer for 30 minutes at high pressure.

Nutrition Facts per Serving
Calories 645, total fat 29 g, carbs 60 g, protein 37.5 g, sodium 2136 mg

Beef and Vegetable Stew

Here is another mouthwatering meat stew to enjoy any time you like.

Servings: 8 – Prep Time: 45 minutes – Cook Time: 35 minutes
Pressure Level: High

Ingredients

4 pounds beef brisket
2 red potatoes, cut into chunks
1 cup cauliflower florets
1 cup carrots, chopped
1 cup onion, chopped
2 cloves garlic, minced
1 teaspoon ginger
Salt and black pepper, to taste
¼ cup olive oil

Directions

1. Turn on the sauté mode of the Crock-Pot® Express.
2. Add oil to the pot and sauté onions until brown.
3. Add ginger, garlic, potatoes, cauliflower, carrots, and beef.
4. Add all the spices and then cook for a few minutes.
5. Secure the lid of the Crock-Pot® Express.
6. Press the MEAT/STEW button and set the timer for 30 minutes at high pressure.

Nutrition Facts per Serving
Calories 535, total fat 21.2 g, carbs 12.2 g, protein 70.4 g, sodium 167 mg

Crock-Pot® Express Meatloaf

The aromatic and delicious ingredients in this recipe take the meatloaf to another level.

Servings: 3 – Prep Time: 6 hours 20 minutes – Cook Time: 6 hours
Pressure Level: low

Ingredients

2 eggs, beaten
½ cup almond milk
½ cup dry breadcrumbs
1 ounce dry onion soup mix
2 pounds lean ground beef

Directions

1. Line the Crock-Pot® Express with aluminum foil all the way up the sides.
2. In a large bowl, whisk together the milk, egg, breadcrumbs, and soup mix.
3. Add the meat and mix together.
4. Make a large rectangle or an oval out of the meat.
5. Place it in the Crock-Pot® Express.
6. Cover and press the MEAT/STEW button.
7. Cook for 6 hours at low temperature and pressure.
8. Remove the loaf and slice it.
9. Serve and enjoy.

Nutrition Facts per Serving
Calories 713, total fat 23 g, carbs 20.7 g, protein 99 g, sodium 1154 mg

Vegetarian Recipes

Hummus Recipe

If you are a lover of hummus, then this recipe is for you!

Servings: 5 – Prep Time: 50 minutes – Cook Time: 45 minutes
Pressure Level: High

Ingredients
4 cups water
1½ cups dried chickpeas
⅓ cup olive oil
2 cloves garlic, peeled
½ cup tahini sauce
⅓ cup water
2 teaspoons lemon juice
1 tablespoon soy sauce
Salt and black pepper, to taste

Directions
1. Pour water into the pot and then add the chickpeas.
2. Secure the lid and press the BEANS/CHILI button.
3. Set the pressure to high and the timer to 45 minutes.
4. Once the timer beeps, release the pressure.
5. Drain the chickpeas and then add them to the blender.
6. Add all the remaining ingredients to the blender.
7. Process to form a paste.
8. Adjust salt and pepper.
9. Serve and enjoy.

Nutrition Facts per Serving
Calories 446, total fat 26.7 g, carbs 39.5 g, protein 14.3 g, sodium 368 mg

Potato Salad

A perfect meal replacement salad recipe that is rich in carbohydrates to fuel the body.

Servings: 8 – Prep Time: 20 minutes – Cook Time: 10 minutes
Pressure Level: High

Ingredients
4 pounds baby potatoes, halved, diced, and peeled
½ cup olive oil
¼ cup white wine vinegar
1 tablespoon mustard
2 cloves garlic, minced
Salt and black pepper, to taste
1 cup tomatoes, sliced and sun-dried
½ cup red onion, minced
4 cups water, for pouring

Directions
1. Pour water into the pot and add the potatoes.
2. Secure the lid of the pot and turn on the Crock-Pot® Express.
3. Press the STEAM button and set pressure and temperature to high.
4. Adjust the timer to 10 minutes.
5. Once the timer goes off, release the pressure.
6. Drain the potatoes using the colander.
7. Let cool slightly.
8. In a bowl, mix oil, vinegar, mustard, garlic, pepper, and salt.
9. Toss in sun-dried tomatoes and red onions.
10. Mix all with the potatoes and then serve.

Nutrition Facts per Serving
Calories 256, total fat 13.3 g, carbs 30 g, protein 6.5 g, sodium 25 mg

Mushroom and Rice

The combination of mushrooms with rice goes really well in this classic recipe.

Servings: 8 – Prep Time: 40 minutes – Cook Time: 30 minutes
Pressure Level: Low

Ingredients

2 tablespoons olive oil
4 cloves garlic, crushed
3 onions, chopped
1 pound Portobello mushrooms, sliced
5 cups Arborio rice
½ cup white wine
7 cups vegetable stock
½ cup parsley, roughly chopped
¼ cup butter, room temperature
Salt and black pepper, to taste

Directions

1. Turn on the sauté mode of the Crock-Pot® Express.
2. Set the temperature to high.
3. Add the oil and cook the onions and garlic for 2 minutes.
4. Add the mushrooms.
5. Cook for 5 minutes, until tender.
6. Add the rice and stir well.
7. Add the wine and allow to cook until reduced to half.
8. Add the vegetable stock.
9. Press the START/STOP button.
10. Secure the lid.
11. Press the RICE/RISOTTO button and set the timer for 15 minutes at low pressure.
12. Press the START/STOP button and release the steam.
13. Fold in the butter and parsley.
14. Adjust the salt and pepper, then serve hot.

Nutrition Facts per Serving

Calories 574, total fat 12.7 g, carbs 104 g, protein 9.3 g, sodium 866 mg

Pumpkin Soup

This is a hit recipe that makes a very healthy soup with very few calories.

Servings: 6 – Prep Time: 5 hours – Cook Time: 4 hours 5 minutes
Pressure Level: High

Ingredients
2 tablespoons butter
3 onions, chopped
4 cloves garlic, crushed
½ cup red curry paste
1 cup coconut cream
1 cup vegetable stock
2 pounds pumpkin, seeds removed, peeled, chopped,
Salt and black pepper, to taste

Directions
1. Turn on the sauté mode of the pot and set the temperature to high.
2. Press the START/STOP button and add onions and butter.
3. Cook for 2 minutes and add curry paste.
4. Cook for one minute.
5. Add all the remaining ingredients to the Crock-Pot® Express.
6. Secure the lid of the pot.
7. Press the START/STOP button.
8. Press SLOW COOK and set the timer to 4 hours on high.
9. Make sure the valve is open.
10. Press START/STOP to start the cooking process.
11. Once cooking is done, make a puree with an immersion blender.
12. Reheat and serve.

Nutrition Facts per Serving
Calories 284, total fat 20.2 g, carbs 24 g, protein 3.4 g, sodium 1203 mg

Veggies Risotto

This very low-calorie meal will keep you full without adding extra calories to the plate.

Servings: 5 – Prep Time: 35 minutes – Cook Time: 22–25minutes
Pressure Level: High

Ingredients
1 onion, diced
¼ cup olive oil
1 fennel, diced
⅓ cup asparagus, diced
Salt, to taste
2 garlic cloves
⅓ cup wine
Zest of ½ lemon
4 cups vegetable soup or stock
1 cup Parmesan cheese, grated

Ingredients to Top the Risotto
2 tablespoons oil
½ fennel
½ asparagus, cubed
⅓ teaspoon salt
½ lemon, juice

Directions
1. Press the BROWN/SAUTÉ button of the Crock-Pot® Express and add the onions and the oil.
2. Sauté until brown.
3. Add the asparagus and fennel.
4. Add the remaining ingredients (excluding the cheese).
5. Lock the lid of the Crock-Pot® Express.
6. Press the START/STOP button.

7. Press the RICE/RISOTTO button and set the timer for 7 minutes at high pressure.
8. In the meantime, heat olive oil in a pan and add all the topping ingredients.
9. Cook for 10 minutes at medium or low heat.
10. Once the timer beeps, release the steam and open the pot by pressing the START/STOP button.
11. Dump in the cheese and stir a few times.
12. Serve it with the pan contents as the topping.
13. Enjoy.

Nutrition Facts per Serving
Calories 332, total fat 21 g, carbs 26.5 g, protein 7.3 g, sodium 891 mg

Coconut Cabbage in Crock Pot

The classic combination of cabbage and coconut milk goes very well with the addition of spices like curry powder and red chili powder.

Servings: 6 – Prep Time: 18 minutes – Cook Time: 10 minutes
Pressure Level: High

Ingredients

2 tablespoons coconut oil
2 red onions, peeled and sliced
Salt, to taste
2 teaspoons garlic, diced
1 teaspoon red chili, sliced
1 tablespoon mustard seeds
2 tablespoons curry powder
½ tablespoon turmeric powder
3 cups cabbage, shredded
2 cups carrot, peeled and sliced
¼ cup lemon juice
1 cup coconut milk, unsweetened

Directions

1. Press the BROWN/SAUTÉ button of the Crock-Pot® Express and turn it on.
2. Preheat the pot and then add the oil, onion, garlic.
3. Cook until aromatic.
4. Add salt, red chili, mustard seed, curry powder, turmeric powder, lemon juice and let cook for a few seconds.
5. Add the carrots and cabbage and pour in the water.
6. Press the START/STOP button and then press the STEAM button.
7. Set the timer for 5 minutes at high pressure.
8. After 5 minutes, release the steam.
9. Open the pot and then add coconut milk.
10. Stir it a few times and then serve.

Nutrition Facts per Serving

Calories 191, total fat 15.1 g, carbs 14.1 g, protein 3 g, sodium 70 mg

Dessert Recipes

Fruits of the Garden

This is a perfect dessert recipe for managing your weight because it doesn't add many extra calories to your diet.

Servings: 6 – Prep Time: 45 minutes – Cook Time: 35 minutes
Pressure Level: High

Ingredients
<u>Main Ingredients</u>
4 plums, peeled, halved, pitted
3 pears, peeled, cored and halved
1 apple, peeled, cored, halved
8 Medjool dates, pitted
14 ounces peaches, sliced
2 cups apricots, sliced
2½ cups black cherries
¼ cup white sugar
⅓ teaspoon cinnamon, grated
¼ cup fresh orange juice

<u>Topping Ingredients</u>
1 tablespoon butter
1 cup almond flour, crushed almonds
⅓ cup walnuts, whole
½ cup macadamia nuts, whole
⅓ cup coconut, shredded

Directions
1. Place all the main ingredients in a Crock-Pot® Express and secure the lid.
2. Press the DESSERT button and then set pressure to high.
3. Set the timer for 30 minutes.

4. Meanwhile, melt the butter in a pan and add all the topping ingredients.
5. Stir for 5 minutes.
6. Once the coconut turns golden brown, turn off the heat and set aside.
7. Once the Crock-Pot® Express timer goes off, press the START/STOP button, open the pot and serve the fruits with the prepared topping.

Nutrition Facts per Serving
Calories 624, total fat 20 g, carbs 116 g, protein 10 g, sodium 21 mg

Chocolate Puddings

This is a yummy treat for all chocolate lovers.

Servings: 4 – Prep Time: 35 minutes – Cook Time: 25 minutes
Pressure Level: High

Ingredients

10 tablespoons butter, melted
⅓ cup brown sugar
1 teaspoon vanilla extract
4 ounces dark chocolate, melted
3 eggs, whisked
½ cup self-rising flour
½ cup plain flour
½ cup cocoa powder
1 cup cream
1 cup milk
2 cups water, for pouring

Directions

1. Grease a small ramekin dish and set aside.
2. To a bowl, add butter, sugar, and vanilla.
3. Add the cream and milk.
4. Whisk the ingredients well.
5. Add the whisked eggs and melted chocolate.
6. Add the flours and the cocoa powder.
7. Mix until formed into a pudding.
8. Fill the greased ramekin with this pudding mixture.
9. Cover the ramekin with foil.
10. Pour 2 cups of water into the Crock-Pot® Express, and then place a steaming rack inside the pot.
11. Place ramekin on top of the steaming rack.
12. Secure the lid of the Crock-Pot® Express.
13. Press the DESSERT button.
14. Start the pot.
15. Set timer for 25 minutes at high pressure.
16. Serve the delicious pudding once cold.

Nutrition Facts per Serving

Calories 652, total fat 46 g, carbs 52 g, protein 12 g, sodium 331 mg

Vanilla Pudding

This is a simple pudding recipe, which is prepared with some of the finest classic ingredients.

Servings: 4 – Prep Time: 35 minutes – Cook Time: 23 minutes
Pressure Level: High

Ingredients
10 tablespoons butter, melted
⅓ cup white sugar
1 teaspoon vanilla extract
3 eggs, whisked
1 cup self-rising flour
½ cup almond flour
1 cup milk
2 cups water, for pouring
1 cup cream

Directions
1. Grease a small ramekin dish.
2. In a medium bowl, mix butter, sugar, and vanilla.
3. Add the cream and milk
4. Whisk the ingredients well.
5. Add the whisked eggs and flours.
6. Mix until you achieve the consistency of a pudding.
7. Fill the greased ramekin with this pudding mixture.
8. Cover the ramekin with the foil well.
9. Pour 2 cups of water into the Crock-Pot® Express, and then place a steaming rack inside the pot.
10. Place the ramekin on top of the steaming rack.
11. Secure the lid of the Crock-Pot® Express.
12. Press the DESSERT button.
13. Start the pot.
14. Set the timer for 23 minutes at high pressure.
15. Serve the delicious pudding once cold.

Nutrition Facts per Serving
Calories 571, total fat 39 g, carbs 46 g, protein 11 g, sodium 304 mg

Poached Pears

This is a very yummy treat to enjoy as a dessert.

Servings: 8 – Prep Time: 20 minutes – Cook Time: 15 minutes
Pressure Level: low

Ingredients
8 Bosc pears, center cored and peeled
4 cardamom pods, crushed
1 clove
2 cinnamon sticks
2 vanilla beans, split
2½ cups red wine
1 cup white sugar
2 tablespoons lemon zest

Ingredients for Cream
1½ cups cream, thickened
2 tablespoons icing sugar

Directions
1. Whip the cream ingredients to make a soft cream for topping.
2. Place the other ingredients in a Crock-Pot® Express.
3. Turn on the pot and press the DESSERT button.
4. Set the timer for 15 minutes at low pressure.
5. Serve the pears with sauce from the pot and prepared cream whip.

Nutrition Facts per Serving
Calories 317, total fat 2.9 g, carbs 63.4 g, protein 1.3 g, sodium 21 mg

Stuffed Apples

These are simple and classic stuffed apples prepared using the Crock-Pot® Express.

Servings: 6 – Prep Time: 20 Minutes – Cook Time: 15 Minutes
Pressure Level: low

Ingredients
6 large baking apples, center cored
1 cup mixed dried fruit
¼ cup honey
½ teaspoon ground cinnamon
½ teaspoon ground nutmeg
¼ cup butter

Directions
1. Grease the sides and center of the Crock-Pot® Express.
2. In a bowl, mix the dried fruits, honey, cinnamon, nutmeg, and butter.
3. Fill the center of the apples with the prepared mixture.
4. Place the apples in the Crock-Pot® Express.
5. Turn on the pot and press the DESSERT button.
6. Set the timer for 15 minutes at low pressure.
7. Serve the apples.

Nutrition Facts per Serving
Calories 298, total fat 8.2 g, carbs 60.2 g, protein 1.7 g, sodium 62 mg

Easy Brownies

This is a very easy brownie recipe, bursting with rich flavors.

Servings: 4 – Prep Time: 30 minutes – Cook Time: 25 minutes
Pressure Level: High

Ingredients
1 packet brownie mix, chocolate
¼ cup butter, melted
½ cup chopped walnuts
2 cups almond milk, as needed

Directions
1. Combine all the ingredients in a bowl, adding milk until a smooth batter is formed.
2. Grease a 6-inch cake pan with oil.
3. Pour the mixture into the pan.
4. Pour 2 cups of water into Crock-Pot® Express, and then place a trivet inside the pot.
5. Place the cake pan on top of the trivet.
6. Secure the lid of the Crock-Pot® Express.
7. Press the DESSERT button.
8. Press the START/STOP button.
9. Set the timer for 25 minutes at high pressure.
10. Allow to cool, then cut and serve.

Nutrition Facts per Serving
Calories 475, total fat 49 g, carbs 8.4 g, protein 6.6 g, sodium 101 mg

Chocolate Chip Peanut Butter Cake

The hit combination of peanut butter and makes this recipe taste divine.

Servings: 6 – Prep Time: 25 minutes – Cook Time: 20 minutes
Pressure Level: High

Ingredients
4 scoops Stevia
4 eggs, whisked
1 cup peanut butter
4 cups self-rising flour
¼ teaspoon salt
1 cup chocolate morsels
2 cups hot fudge, optional

Directions
1. Place a trivet inside the Crock-Pot® Express.
2. Add 2 cups water to the pot.
3. Grease a cake pan.
4. In a bowl, whisk butter with eggs, and then add Stevia, peanut butter, flour, salt and chocolate morsels.
5. Beat well with an electric hand beater.
6. Pour the batter into the greased pan.
7. Place the pan on top of the trivet.
8. Cover the locking lid of the Crock-Pot® Express.
9. Press the DESSERT button and then select high pressure for 20 minutes.
10. Serve with hot fudge sauce and enjoy.

Nutrition Facts per Serving
Calories 947, total fat 30 g, carbs 145 g, protein 25.2 g, sodium 419 mg

Classic Carrot Cake

This is a simple, sweet, and savory recipe to enjoy.

Servings: 6 – Prep Time: 25 minutes – Cook Time: 20 minutes
Pressure Level: High

Ingredients
2 cups almond flour or almond meal
½ cup plain flour
Salt, to taste
6 tablespoons butter
2 cups maple syrup
2 eggs, whisked
2 cups coconut milk
1 teaspoon baking soda
2 cups carrots, grated

Directions
1. Place a steamer basket into the Crock-Pot® Express.
2. Pour two cups of water into the pot.
3. Grease a small cake pan with cooking spray.
4. In a bowl, combine all the listed ingredients to form a batter.
5. Pour the batter into the cake pan.
6. Place the cake pan on top of the steamer basket.
7. Lock the lid of the Crock-Pot® Express.
8. Press the DESSERT button and start the Crock-Pot® Express.
9. Set the timer for 20 minutes at high pressure.
10. Remove the carrot cake from the steamer basket.
11. Let cool and then slice and serve.

Nutrition Facts per Serving
Calories 687, total fat 37 g, carbs 88 g, protein 7.2 g, sodium 387 mg

Recipe Index

Also by Louise Davidson

Here are some of Louise Davidson's other cookbooks.

Appendix - Cooking Conversion Charts

1. Measuring Equivalent Chart

Type	Imperial	Imperial	Metric
Weight	1 dry ounce		28g
	1 pound	16 dry ounces	0.45 kg
Volume	1 teaspoon		5 ml
	1 dessert spoon	2 teaspoons	10 ml
	1 tablespoon	3 teaspoons	15 ml
	1 Australian tablespoon	4 teaspoons	20 ml
	1 fluid ounce	2 tablespoons	30 ml
	1 cup	16 tablespoons	240 ml
	1 cup	8 fluid ounces	240 ml
	1 pint	2 cups	470 ml
	1 quart	2 pints	0.95 l
	1 gallon	4 quarts	3.8 l
Length	1 inch		2.54 cm

* Numbers are rounded to the closest equivalent

2. Oven Temperature Equivalent Chart

Fahrenheit (°F)	Celsius (°C)	Gas Mark
220	100	
225	110	1/4
250	120	1/2
275	140	1
300	150	2
325	160	3
350	180	4
375	190	5
400	200	6
425	220	7
450	230	8
475	250	9
500	260	

* Celsius (°C) = T (°F)-32] * 5/9
** Fahrenheit (°F) = T (°C) * 9/5 + 32
*** Numbers are rounded to the closest equivalent

Printed in Great Britain
by Amazon

25171135R00037

Printed in Great Britain
by Amazon